Saving the Poor House!

Seniors are being ripped off by the government?
Here's the secret for seniors--get reparations tomorrow

This book is intended to put a grimace and then a smile on the faces of almost all seniors. For too long, The most beleaguered citizens in the United States are our senior citizens. Seniors are victims of government fraud and have been since 1980 if not even before that year. It should not be so; but it is easy to explain. There is not one senior citizen member of Congress, who actually depends on Social Security to make their ends meet. How is it then that they get to cast their magic wands annually to determine the SSR COLA increase due seniors. Folks it is the worst annual-fake news that anybody can receive and privately the government, who publishes and calculates this BS laughs at seniors for accepting it.

In this book, I will show how seniors have been defrauded and how each person on Social Security deserves as much as twice what their government check amounts to. You're going to like this book but it may shock you that Uncle Sam is a cheater on the cost of living. That is how this nasty uncle takes money from the pockets of seniors every time he can.

Before the current public govt inflation number (called CPI) of just about 10%, last year in July, when the government said the number was 5.4%, they were lying. Back then the real inflation was 13.5 percent. That is a lot of government cheating but seniors have just been taking it on the chin, not trying to poor mouth the government. Do you know what the number is today. March and April will be worst but as of February the alternate (real) inflation is about 17%. It may even hit the 20% range like in the Carter years.

This fraud on seniors began in the 1980s when the govt realized inflation was costing the treasury a lot of money to keep seniors even. They figured out a scheme to lower COLA and thus the recipient's payments based on adjustments that did not reflect true inflation. So their new CPI is a fraud. It reduces cost of living adjustments and thus budget deficits. This gave the govt a better reading in terms of its expenses. The seniors paid for govt budget control. It was shameful. But the only reason the fraudulent calculations were made was to keep the government payments down. Now, seniors are headed to the poorhouse just to pay the taxes on their homes.

Yes, Congressional inflation estimates unfortunately are bogus. They are intentionally lower than the inflation seniors experience in the stores. Everybody knows it but Congress does nothing about it. There is surely a lot of laughing in Washington at how docile Seniors are each year when they hear about the annual "senior citizens screw job" of the Bureau of Labor Statistics as directed by officials in government. Ask any senior, The amount of the increase doesn't cover even the increase in Medicare so each year, seniors lose purchasing power. Everybody knows it but seniors are so afraid of government they do not complain. That has to end.

Each year nonetheless, seniors receive nothing close to the reality of the real price increases seniors actually pay every-day at supermarkets and clothing stores in America? The law on SSR has been distorted and seniors need and deserve a massive adjustment. It is up to seniors to make sure Congress knows that it has not delivered and seniors are upset about it. Perhaps when seniors are responsible for sending members home for good after the next election, the Congress will understand that message.

If President Obama had another heart, some say it would be lonesome. For eight years, seniors served as the former President's personal punching bag as he stubbornly refused to give seniors a break. Biden is now jabbing the bag making Obama's look small-time. Obama and Biden even tried to reduce senior benefits with his chained CPI proposal. Then, Obama took more than $700 Billion from Medicare to fund his signature legislation known as Obamacare. Democrats, the ones who claim Republicans have no hearts are all Tin Men on the SSR issue and their main man for eight years, Barack H. Obama and now Joe Biden have no regard at all for seniors. Read this book. It will help you get your due from the government.

BRIAN W. KELLY

Title: **Saving Seniors from the Poor House**
Subtitle: Seniors are being ripped off by the government? Here's the secret for seniors--get reparations tomorrow

Copyright © 2022 Brian W. Kelly   Editor Brian P. Kelly
                                         Author Brian W. Kelly

All rights reserved: No part of this book may be reproduced or transmitted in any form, or by any means, electronic or mechanical, including photocopying, recording, scanning, faxing, or by any information storage and retrieval system, without permission from the publisher, LETS GO PUBLISH, in writing.

Disclaimer: Though judicious care was taken throughout the writing and the publication of this work that the information contained herein is accurate, there is no expressed or implied warranty that all information in this book is 100% correct. Therefore, neither LETS GO PUBLISH, nor the author accepts liability for any use of this work.

Trademarks: A number of products and names referenced in this book are trade names and trademarks of their respective companies.

Referenced Material: *The information in this book has been obtained through personal and third party observations, interviews, and copious research. Where unique information has been provided or extracted from other sources, those sources are acknowledged within the text of the book itself or at the end of the chapter in the Sources Section. Thus, there are no formal footnotes nor is there a bibliography section. Any picture that does not have a source was taken from various sites on the Internet with no credit attached. If resource owners would like credit in the next printing, please email publisher.*

Published by: LETS GO PUBLISH!
Publisher: Brian P. Kelly
Editor: Brian P. Kelly
Cover Design: Brian W. Kelly
Mail Location: P.O. Box 621, Wilkes-Barre, PA 18703
Web site   www.letsgopublish.com

Library of Congress Copyright Information Pending

ISBN Information: The International Standard Book Number (ISBN) is a unique machine-readable identification number, which marks any book unmistakably. The ISBN is the clear standard in the book industry. 159 countries and territories are officially ISBN members.

978-1-951562-84-7

The price for this work is : $16.95 USD

10   9   8   7   6   5   4   3   2   1
Release Date: April 2022

Contains Water J Williams'
ShadowStats excerpt
Shows seniors intentionally "screwed" by US
Govt. Isn't it time for seniors to be paid back!

Dedication

*I dedicate this book
To the Kelly Twins, my sister and brother, Mary Daniels
and Joseph Kelly, and their wonderful families*

*They are the youngest members of the Irene and Edward J.
Kelly family.*

*Mary Alice and her husband Bill Daniels are blessed with
three Children and seven grandchildren. Megan and Jason
Kauwell, and their son Nathan and daughter Charlotte;
Elizabeth and Brian Ginochetti, and their daughters Sophia
and Elise, and their son Luke; Billy Daniels, and his son
Jaxen Cole and daughter Skylar*

*Joseph Aloysius and Diane Kelly are blessed with two
daughters and three grandchildren. Tara and Christopher
Bryk, their son Aiden, and their daughter Zoey; Colleen
Kelly and her daughter Caitlin Marie.*

*Hey, don't forget my family, Pat and Brian (mom & dad)
are blessed with Brian Patrick, Michael Patrick, and
Kathleen Patricia. Are we lucky! Yessirree Bob!*

Thank you all for your help and smiles and the best!

Acknowledgments

I would like to thank many, many people for helping me in this effort.

I appreciate all the help that I have received in putting this book together as well as all of my other 286 published books.

My printed acknowledgments had become so large that book readers "complained" about going through too many pages to get to page one of the text.

And, so to permit me more flexibility, I put my acknowledgment list online, and it continues to grow. Believe it or not, it once cost about a dollar more to print each book.

Thank you and God bless you all for your help. In particular thanks are given to Wily Ky Eyeley. Who always approves.

Please check out www.letsgopublish.com to read the latest version of my heartfelt acknowledgments as updated for this book. Click the bottom of the Main menu!

To sum up my acknowledgments, as I do in every book that I have written, I am compelled to offer that I am truly convinced that "the only thing you can do alone in life is fail." Thanks to my family, good friends, and a wonderful helping team, I was never alone.

Table of Contents

Chapter 1 The Government's Hand Is in Your Pocket 1
Chapter 2 Will Social Security Be There for You? 1
Chapter 3 Seniors Have Become Democrat Punching-Bags. 1
Chapter 4 Use Real Inflation v Government Contrivances? 19
Chapter 5 Does Government Lie about Real Inflation? Yes!!! ... 29
Chapter 6 It's Time for "The Seniors Administration." 37
Chapter 7 How Would a Seniors Administration (SA) Help Seniors? 55
Chapter 8 John Williams' Shadow Government Statistics 65
Chapter 9 Social Security "Cheated" Seniors $15,258 in Past Decade 91
Chapter 10 Congress Has Power to Fix Social Security for Seniors 103
Chapter 11 Boost Social Security Right Now! 115
Chapter 12 Hey Buddy; Can You Spare a Dime? 133
Chapter 13 More Proof—System Is Rigged 141
Chapter 14 The Big Question: Is there a Fix? 147
Chapter 15 How to Pay for the Senior SSR Boost? 151
Chapter 16 Senior Solution Review: Pay Back the Big Rip-Off 163
Other Books by Brian W. Kelly: (amazon.com, and Kindle) 167

Preface:

Congress & the President must act now to avoid more seniors perishing in this crisis!

Somebody will say that the US cannot afford to pay for seniors to be OK! I say that we cannot afford not to do what is right, This is America.

Why are retires in other countries not losing their homes to the tax man. Think about that! As you read this book, you will see that I prove beyond the question of a doubt that this debt is owed to seniors and the US has a moral obligation to pay it back to seniors. Sooner rather than later. Additionally, I show where several trillion dollars can come from to make payback not as much of an issue for the government.

If somebody says we cannot afford to assure that seniors can lead lives in which the poorhouse is not a constant threat, please tell them to read almost any part of this book and then use their imagination. We can afford making seniors whole again and we must.

The dirtiest politicians in America colluded so they would not have to take the real cost of living into consideration for the last forty six years or so. Seniors paid by their poor standard of living for what they were cheated by the government.

Nobody in America wants a perpetration against seniors such as this to stand—especially seniors. Politicians know that many seniors are about to lose their homes and who are scraping to find a good meal. The poor house looks more and more like a good option.

For eight years of President Obama's regime, it was not very safe to be a senior citizen. It is still not safe, but many seniors are hopeful that with a new Congress in the fall and a new president (Trump???) in less than three years—in charge, that things will change for the better.

In former President Obama's heart, he had to know that this batch of seniors did not trust him very much to do the right thing by them. Seniors got exactly what they expected from Obama – nothing.

Only low information seniors, and there are far too many for the good of the US senior citizen population, continued to the end to give the former president the benefit of the doubt. For an unexplained reason despite his failings many seniors today will not cast the blame on president Biden. It is Biden's inflation. His fingerprints are on all the bad things happening in America.

I guess too many seniors listen to the corrupt fake-news mainstream media-CNN, MSNBC, ABC, & CBS --and they read the biased v seniors New York Times. All seniors and the rest of America have to wake up. Every family has seniors who depend on SSR benefits. We must all end the cheating perpetrated by a corrupt Congress. Our power comes from our vote. Seniors cannot sit back and be minimized. It is time for seniors to assert their power.

Even today with President Biden destroying the country piece by piece, and many of the pieces are huge, too many starving seniors do not fault the current President or Obama before him. My presumption is that they would scream and kick if they really knew what he did to them.

Worse than that, if they knew how bad he tried to make it, but failed, seniors would be even more enraged. You'll learn what that was in this book. President Obama tried his best to destroy the lives of even more senior citizens than he actually was able to.

It is a documented fact that the most beleaguered citizens in the United States today are senior citizens. Some are so respectful of authority that they become dumb when a Democrat suggests they have it made because of all the great Democratic programs. Try living on that.

Seniors are people in your family and mine. We know our parents and grandparents were not and still are not on the take. They like the idea of Social Security and as my dad would say, "Retirement With Dignity" Seniors are not looking for welfare handouts.

That is why it hurts me as I look at the intentional theft perpetrated upon senior. Instead of using the real rate of inflation which needed no math majors to compute, in the Clinton Administration, agencies of our government were given the OK to figure out ways to make it look like seniors were receiving their due while the government bureaucrats and coffee breath professors in academe added sludge to their calculations to take more away from seniors.

President Roosevelt with Social Security had promised a system in which benefits were to be given in what was supposed to be a constant cost of living increase. Government used the cost of living instead to defraud and cheat seniors out of what was theirs.

Remember, there is a big difference between the satisfaction of a steak and that of a hamburger. There is a big difference between canned tuna fish and cat tuna fish. Yet, somehow the government calculators forget these each fall when they calculate the consumer price index.

A low-ball estimate of the cost to seniors over forty years is more than $2.5 trillion dollars. Now for those hearing this for the first time, it may be easier to understand why seniors are not doing well and why so many are finding they have to give up their family homesteads or not have their next meal. It is tough to believe Americans did this to senior Americans in America. Shame on them.

For eight years, during Obama Times, any senior paying attention noticed that they were serving as former President Obama's personal punching bags. He knew that in their hearts, many, who knew what he was up to had little regard for him.

They had him pegged right as a man who would take away their last drop of water if he could. They were right. There is lots more inside this book to help seniors move to action to assure that SSR increases are fair and that the government immediately brings seniors back to where they should be—after all the government lying on the inflation rate.

Yes, I am talking about a payback for what was stolen from seniors by the government and a restoration of a CoLA based on reality and not hocus pocus calculations. I am also suggesting a new agency called the Seniors Agency be created so that just like the VA helps make sure veterans are not screwed by other branches of the government, the SA would protect seniors. It is time to make it all right for seniors.

If you are a senior or if you have one in your family. you are going to love this book as it tells it like it is. Feel free to contact your Congressman and President so that they know how you feel. One day we will all be seniors. Some of us already are.

I wish you all the best

Brian P. Kelly, Publisher
P.O Box 621 Wilkes-Barre, Pennsylvania 18703

About the Author

Brian W. Kelly is a retired Assistant Professor in the Business Information Technology (BIT) program at Marywood University, where he also served as the IBM i and midrange systems technical advisor to the IT faculty. Kelly developed and taught many college and professional courses in the IT and business areas. He is also a contributing technical editor to IT Jungle's "The Four Hundred" and "Four Hundred Guru" Newsletters. Brian understands numbers which was needed for , with a Masters' Degree in Finance & Accounting, his calculations about what is needed for seniors to become whole are worthy of imitation.

A former IBM senior Systems Engineer, Brian has an active consultancy in the information technology field, (www.kellyconsulting.com). He is the author of dozens of books and numerous articles about current IT topics. Kelly is a frequent speaker at national conferences & user group meetings across the United States. Brian is a 2022 candidate for Congress. briankellyforcongress.com

This is Brian's eighth book about the injustice and dishonesty brought forth upon seniors by an unscrupulous and corrupt Congress. Brian would like to see the look on seniors' faces after you read this book and you find out how much money would be in your monthly payment if Congress had been honest for the last forty years. Kelly is convinced seniors can get a lot of that money back in monthly benefits—if we all insist.

This is Brian Kelly's 295th book.

Chapter 1 The Government's Hand Is in Your Pocket

The invisible hand creates a lot of damage.

In March I gave an interview on WILK Radio. I was a guest on the Frank Andrews' Show. During this appearance, I announced this book. In the interview because I am an honest man, I stated the truth that there is no question that seniors have been the group hardest hit from inflation. Moreover, I noted that the pain has been going on since before 1980 but today, the government's hand that is in your pocket never seems to leave.

Even when they give, they take, It gives with the right hand and takes it back with the left. Joe Biden folks right now is the government. My major announcement in my interview was that that I was in the process of writing this book which as you know is titled: *Saving Seniors from the Poor House.* Don't count on Biden even with help from Obama to provide any relief. In fact, as you inventory all the government hands that are now permanently in your pockets, you will find Joe Biden's His activity creates a huge fingerprint and he removes his hand every so often with a wad of your cash in it.

Biden is not helping Seniors

Biden is not helping seniors. Since 1990 if inflation were calculated correctly, the true CPI would demand that seniors Social Security Payments double. It is probably worse. But don't expect anything. It would be easier for Blacks and American Indians to receive reparations from the government than for seniors who have lost half of their spending since 1990 by jury-rigged fraudulent CoLAs to get even a nickel back. Each year the CoLA reflects less a lower inflation rate as prices go up, real income goes down. This must change or seniors will be in the poor house and somebody else will be living in their homes.

The Seniors coalition think annual 3% raises is enough for seniors. No way, Seniors already get less than half of what they should because of government fraud on the CPI. It's been that way for a long time. 3% is peanuts. 5.9% this year does not come close to this year's 10% inflation rate. We have to make up for lost income while people still live in their family homes.

20% immediate bump

When elected I will propose an immediate 20% increase in Social Security (SSR) payments. This will be followed by additional COLAs of at least 5% every six months for three years and perhaps longer. Also, I will introduce legislation for at least a three year moratorium on Medicare Part B increases. What Brainiac decided that Medicare should be increased to eat up the SSR cost of living increase? Fire that guy!

This new book that you are reading will show that this is not all that is needed but it will be a great start. Why does every country in Europe treat its seniors better than in the US? Why? Because since 1990, they have given real cost of living increases and the US has cheated seniors with a fraudulent CPI.

This book will show seniors that they are always intentionally left out when government decides to help. It is time for seniors to lead the charge to hold our leaders accountable. Let's send home every elected representative that thinks seniors are fat cats. Let's send home every elected representative who thinks seniors do not deserve an immediate 20% increase in Social Security?

Heck we have been adding debt at such a high rate, we could have doubled Seniors checks and not have noticed it. Non-COVID to Covid Times the debt increased by more than $5trillion. That's a lot of COLA increases folks. Seniors deserve them and the US big spenders can pay for it, rather than feed Big Tech

Let's just demonstrate again how seniors get the shaft, the hose job, the bad end of the stick, and nothing to write home about. In January we know that with inflation over 7%, seniors got a 5.9% COLA. Then the government took a third back to pay for Medicare Part B increases and even before the new year began—in the month of December 2021, inflation took most of the remainder. In other words, seniors went negative from a 5.9% raise because of Biden inflation and Biden accounting.

Again seniors are worse off than they were the year before. If we let this happen without complaining my dear fellow seniors, this is a path to the poor-house. There are too many seniors still living to forget seniors. This unfair treatment must end-- and it must end now. As noted, this first 20% boost will not yet bring seniors – even-- with their rising costs but it is a great start. CoLAs of 5% every six months for three years will get us close to where we should be. We may need more. Remember they stole half by their senior-cheating CPI for thirty years.

Seniors are the only ones left out. Meanwhile as we all know, every segment of the population except seniors have been receiving stipends, major pandemic unemployment benefits or substantial increased wages to get them back to work. There have been no special programs or relief for seniors who are losing their homes so they can eat.

Seniors pay these increases to everybody else but get nothing to pay for their own increases. Seniors on fixed income are left with less and because of that, they are all getting closer on their way to the poor house. No more poorhouse. My proposal when enacted will keep seniors from the poor house and bring them back to having some spare change in their pockets on the road to dignity!

Congress looks to the elite Europeans for everything but they don't ask about senior benefits or they'd have to do something about it. The recent Annual Global Retirement Index study by Natixis Investment Managers doesn't even put the US in the top 10. countries. Forty-four countries were evaluated in four key areas: material well-being, health, finances in retirement, and quality of life. The US stunk the house out.

Here are the top 10 countries from top to bottom:

- Iceland
- Switzerland
- Norway
- Ireland
- The Netherlands
- New Zealand
- Australia
- Germany
- Denmark
- Canada

The USA ranks #17, a slight drop from its place at #16 in 2020 and better than being 18th in 2019. The 2021 rating complements a recent survey that found only 41% of Americans believe they'll be able to retire comfortably. It won't get better until seniors start making their wills known. Quiet submission is not working for seniors. It can't work and it won't work. Seniors have to be alarmed and must start screaming bloody murder. Not kidding!

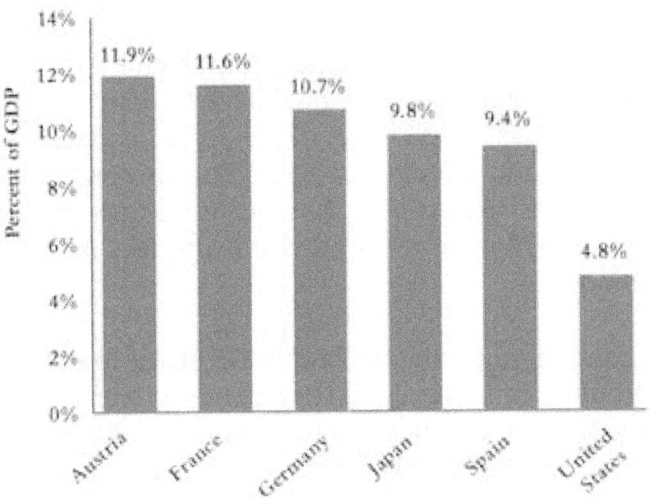

Note: All data are for 2009 (most recent comparative data available). All countries compared have similar, defined-benefit pension systems. Private systems are excluded, as are targeted social assistance programs. To increase data comparability, only half of spending was counted for program components in other countries that cover all government employees (and only a quarter of spending on those that cover a combination of government employees and members of the military/veterans), as only roughly half (a quarter) of such spending in United States is Social Security spending.

Source: Analysis by Benjamin W. Veghte of OECD Social Expenditure Database.

Going back to the times we can remember, Obama was as honest as Biden is honest. What a pair of honest guys??? OK maybe neither of them are honest. Obama claimed he was for seniors but in his spare time, he worked to reduce SSR benefits for the duration of his eight years in office. He holds the miser-record for Social Security with three zero CoLA years out of eight. A real Mr. Generosity???.

Wimpy RINO Republicans without the courage of Donald J. Trump, permitted the former President, back when he did not have a Democrat Majority in Congress to decrease the livelihood of seniors. Too many chose not to fire back with the same gumption they showed when they complained about Trump.

Republicans chose to do nothing to help seniors or President Trump. Mike Huckabee was the first Republican to complain when he publicly accused "illegals, prostitutes, pimps, (and) drug dealers" of freeloading off the Social Security system during the first GOP primary debate way back on August. 6, 2015.

Hey, I am serious. For those in Peoria, that means I am not kidding. This freeloading must be paid back to seniors by the US government. Congress is in charge of the purse no matter what they may say about it. Despite President Trump's problems with Republican RINOs, seniors pray that #45 still wants to help. It seems there is nobody else in government who tells the truth. How does #47 sound?

During his campaign, candidate Trump promised to protect Social Security without cutting benefits. He did; but he was undermined from day one. I wrote this book to help remind the President in his next term or when he gets called back into office when Biden gets the Axe, that the big 20%er and about six huge 5% SSR monthly CoLA bumps over three years and maybe more is about the right medicine and it must be done ASAP before seniors suffer more.

Seniors need to do more than again simply accepting the bad medicine of the past quietly without a peep. Make big peeps! Make big noises to your representatives. These connivers must be paid back for the SSR CoLA abuses over the years that Mike Huckabee and others have cited. If you don't have a mom or a dad who are hurting because their Social Security check does not even pay for their meals, you can't know how bad it is in America for poor seniors.

Folks, poor is not an exaggeration. If you are a poor senior, for goodness sake, speak up, please. Send the Democrat bums that have you on the steps to the poor house, back home to wallow in their own swill. If you don't throw the bums out, there is nobody else.

You know as well as I that just when President Trump was ready to act in the absence of any congressional leadership the Democrats literally stole the election from him. If you don't know that, please ask Mike Lindell and follow his fight for America on OANN. No more Fox News, CNN, or MSNBC.

Trump's positive actions would include paying back Medicare from Obamacare. It would include increasing SSR benefits over the next three or more years of the next Trump term with a 20% immediate CoLA followed by an extra COLA paid twice a year. Even this would not make up for what was stolen from seniors since the first SSR recipient got the first Social Security check.

President Trump knows that revenue flows from elimination of waste, fraud, & abuse and he can direct that American oil spigots get turned on all the way and they will provide ample cash for strategic emergency make-up funding for senior benefits. The seniors cash is in the ground and it is called US Oil and Gas.

For seniors, Trump has lots of ways to pay for the CoLAs. For example, he can also use the $trillion in cash from solving the illegal resident crisis by cracking down on illegal welfare by fake IDs using an innovative resident visa plan. That costs US plenty.

What would you pay to see every senior in America smile because buying a fresh loaf of bread and a dozen eggs would no longer be a big issue in their lives? Seniors ask for nothing more than to be made whole for the intentional fraud perpetrated by an uncaring Congress. They now receive less than half of what they are due in each check.

CPI calculations and in the future CoLAs must use accurate cost of living & out-of-pocket expenses endured by seniors In this book, we show you how they stole the money from seniors and why they think rather than fixing it, they plan to steal more. Hide your wallet when politicians are in the area.

My concern is that the good President Trump, when he again is the sitting as president, hopefully sooner than later, may be so insulated from the reality he knew as a candidate, that he might sit idle and permit an unfair inflation rate put more and more seniors in the poorhouse. Seniors cannot allow that to happen. We must complain and complain loud and send all the bums in Congress home to stay. And make sure that Donald Trump knows he is key to seniors staying out of the poor house.

Trump must make up for all the past bad CPIs in one term all at once. 20% then six iterations of 5% every six months. That will help an awful lot. Seniors are the have-nots and this will help seniors lessen the divide between the haves and have-nots.

America is a wealthy nation. We have the means to take care of our seniors if we so desire. In this book, we tell you how things can and must be made lots better for penniless seniors, whose scant increases get wiped out all the time by Medicare increases. You'll be surprised how much sense Brian Kelly's s solution makes. The President and the Congress cannot be permitted to let seniors down.

Chapter 2 Will Social Security Be There for You?

You bet it will if we elect the right people

Social Security is automatically taken out of employees paychecks at the rate of 6.2% and it is matched by the employer at the same rate of 6.2%. Somehow rich billionaires who like to remain nameless are questioning the unquestionable affordability of Social Security. Amazing! Hearts of stone???

There is apparently a billionaire-funded campaign with huge resources, deploying media savvy agents who have enough money and enough political access to convince Americans that Social Security will not be there for them in the future. Yet from 2020 to 2021, the Government was able to speed through a whopping additional $5Trillion of budget dollars--twice the annual outlay for social security. In this book we show how a huge increase in SSR payments can be afforded regardless of what those nasty billionaires are saying.

Unfortunately this lie of unaffordability is ringing in people's ears and along with other bad ideas and this fake news has been repeated enough, that it has become accepted conventional "wisdom." Makes me want to throw up. How about you? At least the most well-known billionaire of all time Ebenezer Scrooge spent all his time counting his coins rather than trying to spread rumors with the intent of making people's lives more worrisome and miserable.

But somehow certain billionaires like hurting the smallest of us all in our minds if not in our stomachs. We find this big lie distressingly masquerading as conventional wisdom delivering two devastating consequences. Though the anti-Social Security campaign has not succeeded in cutting cash benefits openly, it has eliminated an intangible Social Security benefit.

What a shame that Roosevelt's program that was supposed to provide, as its name indicates, the benefit of security, peace of mind., and other good things like retirement with dignity. Is now a tool for anti SSR and anti-senior propagandists. Despite their minimal success, polls show that too many Americans believe that Social Security is unaffordable and so it cannot possibly be there for them in the future. Who does it help for these rich billionaires if you'll forgive my redundancy, to create angst among those whose endowments don't necessarily qualify as endowments.

People will always have a reason to find something to worry about—especially those who watch as inadequate CoLAs, Medicare increases, and Biden inflation take their meager savings and diminish it without any benefit to the holder. Moreover, perhaps not surprisingly, numerous surveys show that not having enough money in retirement continues as one of the top financial concern of most Americans.

It is an even higher concern than, for example, being able to pay medical bills in the event of a serious illness or the concern of not being able to pay for college. The EMTALA law requiring hospitals to take and care for all patients helps ease the fear of the former whereas college is getting a negative reading nowadays as college students appear too often to behave as anti-American.

Not to change the story but to explain the diversion, last summer as a small example, a group of Georgetown University students said they were "embarrassed" to be American in shocking campus interviews when most people were donning patriotic garb ahead of the July 4 holiday weekend. Despite decrying the Constitution and the Bill of rights including the 2nd amendment, none of the interviewees could name a better country to live in. Humph!

Moreover, this lie of unaffordability, promoted by the elitists in this campaign has seemed to cause gridlock and blocked progress. Instead of a productive debate about the desired level of benefits and the fairest way to allocate the costs for seniors to survive, , the lie of unaffordability has caused the elite conversation over the last twenty years to focus on how politicians can cut Social Security without getting thrown out of office. They are sneakily trying every day. The fact is that without John Williams and a few others out there, with Shadowstats, for example, the answer is that they can't make it much worse than they already have.

Social Security does not provide Americans with the same lifestyle as the European countries who seem to value their elderly much more than the winy liberal Marxists in America. Even though they know Americans are not getting rich on SSR, as the benefits are quite modest, they still seek to reduce them. They won't admit it in public however. When pressed, even they will readily admit the SSR benefits proven to be vitally important to senior sustenance.

The SSR benefits package are most Americans' most significant, and often only, retirement annuity, life insurance and disability insurance. Those benefits account for more than half the income of four out of five people receiving disability insurance, and two out of three seniors receiving retirement benefits. Think about how significant this meager, quite modest amount, actually is. If you have seniors in your family, or you are a senior, you already know

The benefits account for virtually all of the income of one-third of senior and disability beneficiaries. And the children who receive Social Security live in families with considerably fewer resources, on average, than other families with children. Moreover, though created to allow workers to maintain their standards of living and so prevent, rather than alleviate poverty, Social Security nevertheless lifts over many million Americans, including over a million children, out of poverty, and lessens the depth of poverty for millions more. It is very important for sure but it is not enough.

Being elderly is like having a gender or a religion, or an ideology. Everybody gets old except those with early diseases that are killers. It is up to all Americans to support the elderly and for the billionaires to stop whining about not having enough money for social security recipients. American can afford whatever we choose. What we cannot afford is the billionaire's desire to abandon the elderly. In fact we need to do more and that is what this book is all about.

Furthermore, Social Security benefits are projected to be even more important to future generations of beneficiaries, as a result of the disappearance of private sector traditional pensions and their replacement by the grossly inadequate 401(k) savings plans. These plans go down as a totally failed government experiment.

Classic Poor House

As a consequence of those and other factors, the nation is facing a looming retirement income crisis, where most workers will be unable to cease work without a drastic reduction in their standards of living. Over half of American households headed by someone of working age will not be able to maintain their standards of living in old age, and this figure rises to roughly two-thirds when health and long-term care costs are also considered.

With all the oil and gas in the ground in the US – ground owned by the American public, a prudent use policy can be very effective in saving seniors by funding adequate CoLAs. This is an easy way for America to keep seniors out of the poor house.

Particularly after President George W. Bush's failed efforts, feckless and uncaring policymakers realized that, given the importance and popularity of Social Security, cutting Social Security in the sunshine was not an option. They hoped that it could be done through undemocratic fast tracking of legislation crafted behind closed doors, away from the eyes of the American people and the groups of big shots in Washington that represent them.

Notwithstanding their years of trying, though, this didn't work completely. The many nameless, faceless, ineffective, biased "trustees" of the system simply could not pull it off. Shadowstats can prove that SSR payments are less than half of what they would be if the policymakers had been honest caretakers of what in some cases is our parents social security funds. It is hard to believe that these billionaires can't say enough is enough and won't begin to work to make it better for their parents and their parents' parents.

One thing is for sure, the plight of seniors in 2022 is intentional and has been coming for a long time. The "trustees" knew this was inevitable. The good people of America have to take a stand. Seniors have to vote out the perpetrators, aka the Congress, who support the poor house lobby.

Before the pandemic began, the "Trustees" estimated that Social Security's combined trust funds would run out of money by 2035, at which point they claim, benefit cuts would be on the table. Well, not on my table and not on your table either! Seniors must be treated better than commodities. This conclusion of inevitability is at best bulldinky, and that is a kind word to describe the anti-senior lobby. This should never happen and with the proper representation thoughts like this will never reach the light of day.

Nonetheless the billionaires ask you to prepare for the inevitable. I say prepare by cleaning out the Congress of all the anti-seniors. *Pro Senior* is my new litmus test. If you are anti-senior, get out of politics as you will never get elected again.

Their timeline has since been moved up. Now, the untrustworthy billionaires and "Trustees" are saying that because of widespread unemployment during the pandemic, Social Security's trust funds will be depleted by 2034. And once that happens, seniors may be looking at a 22% benefit cut. Get out of town! Rest assured that it will never happen if seniors speak up.

For current retirees who are very reliant on Social Security, that's extremely frightening and problematic. In America, again we can do anything we have a mind to do. "Screwing seniors" is one thing we cannot permit to ever be on the table.

The deadlock and lack of progress created by the lie of unaffordability is now poised to be broken, however. Fortunately, at the same time that some in Washington continue to seek to cut Social Security behind closed doors, others were and continue to work constructively. Again we the names of our opponents so we can remove them. When Obama needed to get reelected, even he recognized it was impossible without the support of seniors.

Let's face it when Obama announced he was for expanding Social Security, he was not being altruistic. After he was elected he proved it was just rhetoric. But the fact is folks, if SSR payments can be justified to be expanded, surely the system can be afforded.

If we can shut up the whiny negative billionaires long enough, the fact is that expanding Social Security is profoundly wise policy and it is also a winning politics strategy. It is a powerful combination if we can keep the billionaires from whining and crying at the celebration party. Let's send them home.

It is a fact that over the last few years, the idea of expanding Social Security has become a steadily growing movement within the Democratic Party. Republicans would be wise to get on board as a major positive that seniors will remember and they will never forget who helped the most.

So, what is the bottom line? Now that the lie of unaffordability is increasingly being exposed, the debate can become an honest one. It can become, as it should be, a debate about values and what kind of country we want. Once the debate is no longer distorted by the false premise that we must cut Social Security, the questions will become unbiased.

Should Social Security be expanded or cut? What is the fairest way to distribute the cost of the level of benefits agreed upon? My plan of an immediate 20% increase followed by at least 5% every six months for at least three more years is sound and doable. Whoever gets their name on that proposal—Republican or Democrat will be sent back to Congress forever.

Other than the hard-hearted and the whining billionaires, it is an easy debate, as well. The American people are overwhelmingly united. Poll after poll shows that Americans support Social Security, believe it is more important than ever, would like to see its benefits increased, adamantly oppose cuts to those earned benefits, and believe that, given how much of the nation's wealth has flowed to those at the top, the wealthiest among us are the ones who should pay more. They should not be whining or conniving to reduce seniors' benefits forcing them to the poor house.

This debate can and should be held in the sunshine, through the regular legislative process as has been the case historically with respect to important Social Security legislation. Republicans need to get on board quickly or it will be political suicide. Democrats are looked upon right now as the scum of the earth trying to destroy America. If Republicans are proven to be against seniors, they won't get elected dog catcher in most places. It is political suicide for any party to be against seniors when seniors choose to unite.

Unfortunately, so far, because of the effectiveness of the unaffordability lie, Americans, especially seniors, have not been presented with a clear electoral choice on the issue of Social Security for too many years. Buying the lie that the program had to be cut, politicians routinely talked of the need to "save" Social Security and vaguely urged a "bipartisan solution." Democrats and Republicans were indistinguishable, since both sides used the same rhetoric. It is up to seniors to start taking names.

By loudly and boldly advocating the expansion of Social Security, smart politicians from both parties need to advocate for the cementing of a powerful, important Social Security legacy that will follow in the best traditions of the American way. I think when the political actors realize that there is a race to get credit for taking care of seniors, in no time both parties will be making "no poorhouse for seniors" a campaign slogan in both parties.

The pro senior lobby can have a profound impact on the issue of support for seniors in all presidencies. It may be too late for Biden but maybe not if he can preach consistency and show he means business by immediately giving seniors the 20% bump in benefit payments as I prescribe.

A bully pulpit will help but seniors will not accept bullcrap in completing the process of converting the Social Security debate back into an honest one about values and competing visions of the future. Would it not be great, as well as right and just if sometime soon we saw Democrats and Republicans singing the same tune on seniors. 20% immediately, and 5% every six months for at least three years. It is that simple You won't be able to wipe the smile from a senor's face.

Whoever says it first will be the immediate political winner; but the other side, if they expect to be relevant in the political future; would need to adopt or top the "no poorhouse for seniors" bandwagon for it will be playing a tune for seniors and for

America's goodness as a country. Anybody who can't dance will be out of the picture.

Republicans for my money right now are too quiet on the subject. This is the sixth book I have written about taking care of seniors so the great thoughts on how to best treat the problem of the poorhouse have been well explored. Now is the time for action.

Republicans, in order to assure what should be a shoe in victory this year, must beat Democrats to the punch. To show that the Republican party is serious about values and goodness to the elderly, Republicans need to talk up their plan to immediately give seniors the 20% bump in benefit payments as I prescribe followed by six 5% payments over three years, and perhaps even more to come.

Doing this will give Republicans, who have the game if they want it in 2022, the historical edge for Social Security benefits will be recognized as the biggest GOP win ever. It will be forever important and lasting. With this one action, the Republicans will have paved the way for a future President, say Donald Trump in 2024, along with a 2022 Republican-dominated Congress. As long as the perception is that the Republicans were the party that increased the economic security of working families by expanding Social Security.

If the GOP Party stalwarts such as Ronna McDaniel, the current RNC Chairwoman, and viable candidates can beat the Dems to the punch on this major lift to seniors, they will become unbeatable. That is a powerful legacy that will benefit hundreds of millions of Americans, now and in the future. All of those Americans are potential voters.

Chapter 3 Seniors Have Become Democrat Punching-Bags.

Just like Bob sucker punched Dr. Marvin,

seniors need a break-away moment

2 What About Seniors?

What about Seniors? Can Hollywood give us the answer? Do Hollywood Democrats care at all? After all, there is no doubt the Hollywood writers wrote a fine ending to solve the vexing problem in that hit movie *What About Bob?*

Well, what about seniors?

Bob was not too big a problem for Hollywood's experienced writers. So shouldn't seniors be an easier issue to solve? In one of their most amusing plots of the century, Hollywood created a successful psychotherapist who loses his mind after one of his most dependent patients, an obsessive-compulsive neurotic, tracks him down during his family vacation. Start laughing now. Better yet, see the movie. Many reading this book are starring in their own movie "What about Seniors?"

A little more detail on Bob would help. Before going on vacation, self-involved psychiatrist Dr. Leo Marvin (Richard Dreyfuss) has the misfortune of taking on a new patient: Bob Wiley (Bill Murray). A paragon of neediness and a compendium of phobias, Bob follows Marvin to his family's country house. Dr. Marvin tries to get him to leave. The trouble is everyone loves Bob. They would rather get rid of the good doctor. As his oblivious patient makes himself at home, Dr. Marvin loses his professional composure and, before long, seems to be ready for the loony bin himself.

The family is like the Democrats who conspired to put Seniors in the poorhouse and just like they continue to pretend there are no ways to bring back the money they stole from the "fund," the family never finds a way to get rid of Bob? It seems that complaining does not help Dr. Marvin,.

So far, complaining has not helped Seniors get back a dime or better yet, get back on the proper greenback track from all the dollars stolen since 1940—ant there are lots someplace. Would you believe me if I told you that Bob actually crossed over to our lives and he stole all the money from the Social Security Lockbox. Or was that uncle Barack or uncle Joe?

Am I the only person who knows how to get it back? Pay attention to this book if you are a senior and you can learn the secret also, You may never get rich but you can get out of the deep part of the poorhouse.

If you are looking for a parallel so a lesson can be learned from the two stories -- What about Seniors! & What About Bob? the parallel is that Wiley (Bob) was dependent on Leo (Marvin) and felt he couldn't survive without him. It was Wiley who made himself dependent on Marvin. Marvin didn't really care about Wiley as he was only a source of funds (psychiatry fees). If the government didn't really have a fund (they actually do not) they would be further restricted in borrowing. The fund is someplace out there stuffed with T-bills (IOUs) from your contributions controlled by the people you voted for. In this book we tell you how to claim your share that the government stole.

Retirees receiving Social Security are suckers for believing in the government. My dad told me Social Security was "invented" to have the people contribute to their own retirement with dignity. He did not realize Lyndon Baines Johnson had other uses for the funds and he had the first key to the lockbox.

Former Senator Jim DeMint wrote in one of his books titled Now Or Never, "Raiding the Social Security Trust Fund was a precedent set in 1968 by another progressive president, Lyndon B. Johnson, to help pay for the Vietnam War." Let me ask the seniors out there—do you trust the government?

Seniors continue to feel pressure on their standard of living because government has been a dishonest caretaker of the public's retirement money. The fact is that the Congress makes it worse by purposely miscalculating the true inflation rate using gimmicks instead of reality. The result is that even with a higher-than-average cost of living increase. Social Security benefits typically do not keep up with the everyday expenses retirees face as they age. The folks, especially seniors, pay the price but seniors have a tough time believing their favorite Democrats would ever be cheating them. We are talking real expenses seniors must pay to live. Seniors are too nice to blame the thieves.

How about livings expenses like rent, food, transportation (including gas), and of course, health care and the astronomical amount of money people must pay for life-saving prescription drugs. How do I know this? From the research I have done for the seven previous books about my recommended boosting of social security, I have become one of the most knowledgeable sources on the subject who ever lived.

Here are the books including this one and those from previous research along with the year published :

- ✓ **Saving Seniors from the Poorhouse April 2022**
- ✓ **What about Seniors? August 2021.**
- ✓ **Social Security Screw Job 2020**
- ✓ **Government Must Stop Ripping Off Seniors' Social Security!: 2019**
- ✓ **Solved II! Jan 31, 2018** Social Security Recipients
- ✓ **Boost Social Security Now Nov 28, 2017**
- ✓ **President D.J. Trump, Time for Seniors to Get a Break Feb 2, 2017**
- ✓ **Seniors, Social Security, & the Minimum Wage. Sept 29, 2016**

What is the biggest truth to support my claim? Consider the fact that The Social Security Act was signed into law by President Roosevelt on August 14, 1935. In addition to several provisions for general welfare, the new Act created a social insurance program designed to pay retired workers at age 65 or older a continuing income after retirement. It was about five years later on January 31, 1940 that the first dime was paid from the fund.

The recipient was Ida May Fuller. From Ida May Fuller's Payroll Tax Contributions and the contributions of others over those five or so years, the fund was able to begin making payments to retirees, Just five years after Roosevelt signed the bill, on January 31, 1940, the first monthly retirement check was issued to Ida May Fuller of Ludlow, Vermont, in the amount of $22.54. How much would that $22.54 cents a month payment amount to on January 31, 2021?

Calculating the Date difference from Jan 31, 1940 (1st SSR check) to Aug 21, 2021 (today)

The total number of days between Wednesday, January 31st, 1940 and Saturday, August 21st, 2021 is 29,788 days.

This is equal to 81 years, 6 months, and 21 days.
This does not include the end date, so it's accurate if you're measuring your age in days, or the total days between the start and end date. But if you want the duration of an event that includes both the starting date and the ending date, then it would actually be 29,789 days.

Unfortunately, the cheap (no cost) inflation calculators on the Internet work only with whole years. So let's use 1940 through 2021 knowing we will be short a few bucks. SSR recipients are short a lot of bucks right now.

$22.40 in 1940 is equivalent in purchasing power to about $436.80 today, an increase of $414.40 over 81 years. The calculator uses a dollar with an average inflation rate of 3.74% per year between 1940 and today, producing a cumulative price increase of 1,850.02%. I did not try to assure the inflation rate.

This means that today's prices are 19.50 times higher than average prices since 1940, according to the Bureau of Labor Statistics consumer price index. A dollar today only buys 5.13% of what it could buy back then.

The 1940 inflation rate was 0.72%. The current year-over-year inflation rate (2020 to 2021) is now 5.37% If this number holds, $22.40 today will be equivalent in buying power to $23.60 in 2022. The current inflation rate page gives more detail on the latest inflation rates.

Let's now use the Accurate Historical Inflation Calculator

This Historical Inflation Calculator will calculate the amount of CPI price inflation between any two dates from 1913 up to the latest month reported by the U.S. Bureau of Labor Statistics (BLS).

The CPI data is sourced from the BLS. However, we also present our own "Alternate Shadowstats" CPI (the real cost of living) estimates for comparison purposes.

Further background on the SGS-Alternate CPI series is available in the Shadowstats Public Comment on Inflation Measurement. Note that we show the Alternate SGS estimates graphically for non-subscribers, and with numerical precision for subscribers.

Shadowstats, which we will discuss in detail in this book, is an alternate (real) way to figure out the inflation rate. Consider this when calculating how the government has short-changed seniors by using various tools known as consumer price indexes, which are engineered to give the government some of your money each year by not using the real cost of goods in the inflation rate. However, the shadowstats alternate index gives a true reading.

Here is how much a senior living in 1940 collecting SSR has lost to today. Yes, I know there are not too many people from 1940 left if any but it shows the rip-off employed by our government.

Inflation Calculator

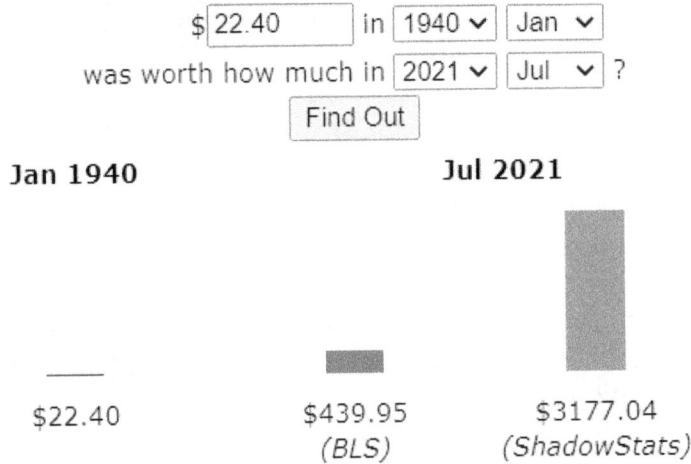

BLS: Bureau of Labor Statistics, CPI-U (Urban Workers, All Items).
ShadowStats: Shadow Government Statistics Alternate CPI.

What this means folks is that a dollar in 1940 is today worth $141.83. Yes, that means a dollar is worth 141.83 times less now than in 1940. The first SS check given out was $22.40. If that check were invested at the Shadowstats alternate rate, it would be worth $3177.04 today. In other words, if the government adjusted COLA with a rea cost of living index, Ida May Fuller would be collecting a check in the amount of $3177.04 every month using true inflation.

If the same $22.40 that Ida collected in 1940 were adjusted by the Consumer price index as used in the Bureau of Labor Statistics, the monthly check would be 439.95 which is 7.22 times less than the amount she would have been collecting if the government used a real cost of goods number in their inflation statistics. Ida would have been ripped off by 722%.

Let's look at the average Social Security check from 1990. Today 31 years later this would be worth which was 550.50

Jan 1990   **Jul 2021**

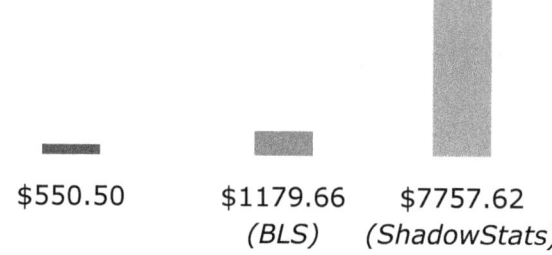

$550.50 $1179.66 $7757.62
              (BLS)   (ShadowStats)

The BLS number (1179.66) is what you would be receiving in your Social Security check. If the real cost of goods was used as the check determinant, you would be receiving $7,757.62 per month. That is a huge discrepancy because the government uses a bogus method to calculate inflation to keep your check amount a lot lower. $7,757.62 v $1179.66.

I bet you knew you were being ripped off but not by so much. The government shortchanged your check by a factor of 6.57 or 657 percent. In real dollars your check is shortchanged by $6577.96. I bet you could use that money now rather than be teetering on the verge of poorhouse residency.

For those who have been on SSR for ten years since July 2011, let's see how much you lost on your last paycheck.

The average SS check in 2011 was 1183.50. Let's see what that computes to with inflation by 2021 using this special calculator:

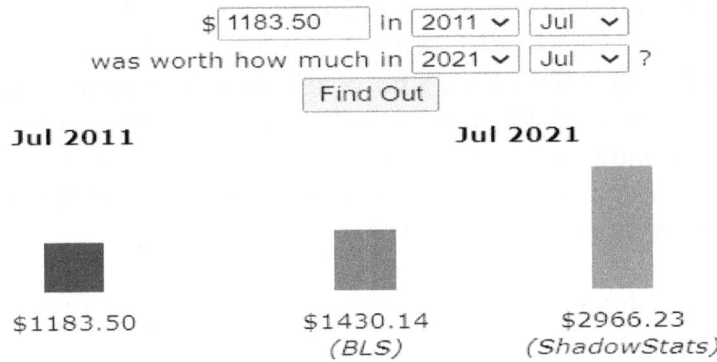

BLS: Bureau of Labor Statistics, CPI-U (Urban Workers, All Items).
ShadowStats: Shadow Government Statistics Alternate CPI.

As you can see, in ten years from 2011 to 2021, the average SSR check increased to $1430.14 from $1183.50 = a 246.64 per check gain instead of a 1782.73 per check gain. The 2966.23 amount is real inflation considered. That is real money folks. The check amount should have almost tripled. Who gets the money you lost. The government. Can they pay you back? Would they if they could?

The Democrats have already spent about $6 trillion in 2021's budget. I think they could afford to pay seniors back for what they stole. Don't you?

Maybe senior citizens do not matter to Democrats?

Picture granny being pushed off a cliff. Then remember those were all Democrat "feel-good" ads. But nobody felt good. Democrats have no love affair with seniors and have been trying to scare the elderly from time immemorial. It is the Democrat bureaucrats and the coffee-breath professors in Democrat-infested academe who have stacked the CoLA deck against seniors as they try to do whatever they can to reduce Social Security Retirement (SSR) benefits on the backs of seniors.

Though SSR is indexed for inflation, the index according to the senior citizens league is a ***designed rip-off of seniors***. The government is intentionally taking money from seniors and claiming that all is well. Here's how they do it. If you ever forget that just reread the shadowstats calculations as it is real money folks. It is money that would have kept many seniors out of the poorhouse. If you are not yet in the poorhouse it is not because the Democrats have not tried.

The below reality CoLAs are having a significant impact on lifetime Social Security income and the standard of living of retirees, particularly those who have been retired since 2009. According to an analysis by TSCL's Social Security policy analyst, Mary Johnson, Social Security benefits are about 17.5 percent lower today than they would have been if the CPI were calculated fairly. Over ten years that's about $17,299 less in retirement income for someone with average benefits," Johnson notes.

Because low CoLAs compound over time, this loss of income due to low COLAs will continue to grow deeper as beneficiaries age. "This has not gone unnoticed by those who depend on these annual adjustments," she says. "Many Social Security recipients tell us their standard of living has declined," Johnson says. For some, feeding the family has become an almost impossible task because the government has stolen money from seniors. We prove our point in this book.

The Obama years were the worst for seniors. Democrat leadership simply are anti-senior and have been since I can remember. Ask them and be prepared for a lie that if you can remember it, you and your family can enjoy forever. You surely will not get the truth.

With CNN, an anti-senior media network, as their only guide, I regret that most Democrats cannot recognize the truth. I mean even if the mere recognition of the truth were part of an entrance exam for a post-mortem admission into heaven as a spirit, CNN & Democrat leaders would fail. Liars are not welcome in God's land.

Chapter 3 Seniors Have Become Democrat Punching Bags.

Do you recall back in 2018, with AOC running the Party, Democrats announced their plan to water down Medicare, a great program which works well for all seniors. Their idea back then was to use the almost-bankrupt system to make Medicare benefits available for non-seniors including illegal aliens. Democrats love giving other people's money (OPM) away to the under deserving.

It would not matter if you paid in a dime or a million dollars. Dems want to give everything to everybody else for free. They are happy getting credit for solving the health problems of every other country in the world if their citizens can sneak into the US.

Democrats are A-OK with payments to illegals bankrupting the system as they believe regular Americans have it too good and illegals are entitled to taking cash from the wallets of Americans. If Medicare went bankrupt in the process, it would serve Americans right according to Democrats who believe there is no reason Americans should have it so well when illegals and those on welfare are struggling. That's how Democrats think.

You may recall former White House counselor Kellyanne Conway slammed Democratic congressional candidate Alexandria Ocasio-Cortez (AOC) over her calls for "Medicare for all." Conway told senior citizens not to be "fooled" by their health care plan.

"Seniors don't be fooled, it is anti-senior, anti-choice," Conway said during an appearance on "Fox and Friends" during this time period.

"You'll lose your doctor; it'll destroy Medicare Advantage, and I know Alexandria Ocasio-Cortez couldn't say what it would cost so let me help her out again: About $32 trillion is the estimate of its price tag," Conway added. In essence, by enacting Medicare for all, the one health plan that works for seniors, Medicare, will be virtually eliminated.

It is amazing that Democrats fail to recognize senior citizens as an important voting bloc, yet illegal aliens are very important to them. Look at today's mad dash to the southern border.

For example, it is amazing that in the Democrat national debates that Joe and Kamala won, not one moderator asked the taboo question about how the presidential wannabes would secure Medicare's finances and keep the promise the nation has made to seniors on constant inflation dollars. It's as if people 65-and-over simply do not count. It's like nobody is thinking about seniors simply because for Democrats, seniors are not really important, unless they are non-citizens.

The truth is for Democrats, seniors do not count. In contrast, for your information, former President Donald Trump, who the Dems will lie about whenever their lips are moving, showing the President pushing granny off a cliff roots for seniors, He was on the side of seniors for his entire four years. As we approached the year 2021 when Trump had the reins, despite the lies of Democrats, Trump had already taken steps to avert Medicare's meltdown but Biden reversed just about all his initiatives. Memorializing this fact, Real Clear Politics recently penned a fact-based article entitled:

"Democrats to seniors: *Drop Dead.*"

I studied the plight of seniors trying to make ends meet and I can say things are not close to easy for our nation's elderly. More and more are losing their homes every year that goes by. I have learned too well just how appalling it is. First of all, there was a zero Social Security (SSR) CoLA for years with rampant inflation raging. Such conditions have made it hard for the elderly to make various payments and their many taxes are unsustainable. The government was simply cheating seniors. I know it is hard to believe—at least it was until recently when every other word from Biden's mouth is a lie.

Plus, those who collect mortgage payments and credit card payments and any credit payments and kind of credit loans—are permitting less and less time for seniors for slightly overdue late payments. The bill collectors make more money when seniors default than when they pay on time. So the modus operandi is to snatch the property while seniors are anticipating relief. There are big profits in the business of taking people's homes.

What I am saying is that people are not as kind as they once were and the elderly are not given as much consideration as in the past. By checking Shadowstats inflation (http://www.shadowstats.com/), you can readily see the dollars the government has literally stolen from seniors. How did they get away with it? Seniors grew up in better times and are way too trusting of the people who now run the Democrat Party.

There is also a lot of hate out there. Democrats do their best to frighten seniors who do not still pay homage to Barack, Hillary and now Joe Biden and Nancy Pelosi. They did their best work with the four years of fake Russia, Russia, Russia for seniors to reject President Trump. Now we know based on Hunter's laptop and the Durham report that Hillary Clinton paid for it all (with foundation money of course.)

Besides cold hearted crooked Hillary and sleepy and nasty Joe Biden, less people give others a chance to get OK in life. Seniors are last on the Democrats list but they talk a good game.

Lending institutions are making matters way worse by preying on seniors who are vulnerable. Even if they miss by a little bit or they don't file paperwork right on time, or they fall behind on insurance, it can signal the end of leniency, and poof--they lose their house—no matter how long they may have lived there. Then what? It is part of the new game. Seniors do not count in the land of Democrats.

Unscrupulous lenders are like buzzard hawks driven to move swiftly to foreclose on homes. These foreclosures have been wiping out hard-earned "generational wealth" built in the decades since the Fair Housing Act of 1968. As bad as it is for seniors because their proper COLA never arrives, conditions make it worse simply because they are old and vulnerable, and there is no agency that assures that they get a fair shot in life.

Congress had not been motivated to help seniors.

There is plenty of opportunity to solve this for those running for high level offices in the Federal Government. Those running for Congress and the US Senate and of course the office of the president could solve this by jointly working together for a solution that makes things right for seniors. As you know by now, my recommendation is a quick fix of a 20% immediate Cola for all seniors except those who tell Congress they don't need it. This would be followed by three years of Cola at 5% above the government's CPI.

Considering that we now have proof that many seniors are receiving 1/3 the % value of a dollar from Roosevelt's enactment of Social Security. In other words, instead of $100, they receive $34.00. They have been cheated out of $66.00 for every hundred they are owed. So, don't say the government does not have the money to pay seniors. This is a big lie perpetrated by whiny billionaires. With one 20% bump immediately followed by six 5% bumps over three years, seniors will only approach receiving what they are really due and have been due for many years. Congress should not wait another minute to supply such reparations to seniors Social Security Accounts.

No more starving for seniors. No more fear of the poorhouse.

If candidates looking to win the next election would look at senior issues and offer real solutions for seniors, such a *real candidate platform package* for seniors, it would be a winning strategy for anybody wanting to make a difference and without a doubt, they would win the next election. It is a chance for potential federal government officials to promise to make things right for seniors. The package of changes we recommend in this book would give any candidate for Congress, the Senate, or the Presidency a decided edge.

The recommendations I would place in any set of winning-platform talking points would be designed to stop this travesty of fraudulent COLAs for seniors in the future and assure that seniors get things moving in their direction for the first time since Roosevelt was president.

Besides stopping the ridiculous tax on SSR benefits; seniors need their own advocacy agency; plus a one-time catch-up-period for past COLA amounts fraudulently denied. Seniors must also demand a return to a real inflation index not an estimate based on Kentucky Windage.

The billionaire trustees and the government employees in the Bureau of Labor Statistics (BLS) should be ashamed of stealing from seniors by producing a fake CPI, instead of using the constant inflation rate that Roosevelt promised SSR recipients.

Such government cheating has cost seniors well into the multiple thousands of dollars. The government needs to look hard at Shadowstats (http://www.shadowstats.com/) so that they understand that just one extra-large COLA would not even come close to paying back seniors for that they are owed. Having said that, it would surely help those on the verge of foreclosure to both eat and keep their homes

To repeat the quick fix, is 20% immediately, and 5% for the next three years, once every six months.

Since nobody is looking after the elderly on Social Security, the nations' seniors need the fake government estimates concocted by the corrupt BLS to be deemed illegal. Quite frankly, seniors need a presidential and congressional focus on providing a fair shake in the future—without seniors having to wait for the hereafter for a better life.

Since the Carter years ,when senior citizens first became the punching bags for Congress—with all the bureaucrats together working to reduce Social Security benefits—a number of government punches, such as the yearly deceitful CoLA has really pounded seniors hard. It has impacted their ability to find the funds necessary to make ends meet.

16 What About Seniors?

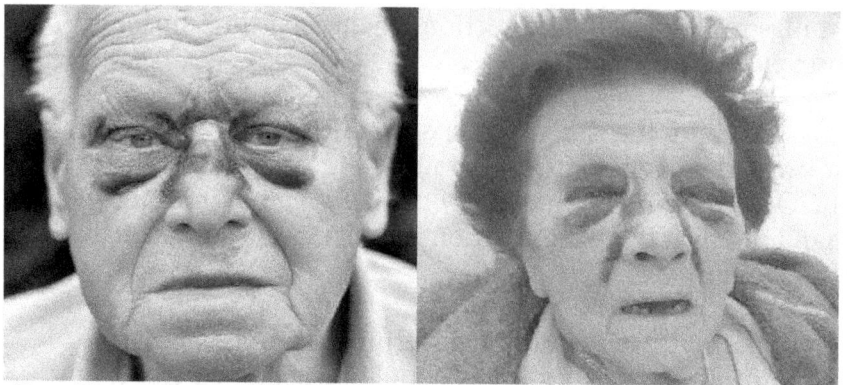

Two Democrat punching bags above have taken big hits from government

COLA calculations are intentionally fraudulent

Studying the history of the Social Security Retirement Benefit (SSR) cost of living adjustment (CoLA) and the Bureau of Labor Statistics (BLS)-contrived consumer price indexes (CPI-W), fairness clearly was never the objective. From Jimmy Carter's presidency through Barack Obama's, it became obvious that seniors no longer would have to buy big pocketbooks for their minimal adjustments. Even Obama did his best not to fill the small coffers kept by seniors. The Obama years were really tough on seniors.

You probably know already but not because seniors are complainers that no less than three times during his presidency, President Obama, not known to be a great lover of seniors, "gave" SSR recipients a zero COLA during tough inflationary times.

Then, in 2016, Obama's last opportunity to do right by seniors, which was also his last year before Trump, he failed Americans again. When many thought that finally after such lean years, a big COLA would be coming from the Obama presidency—there was another zero increase in 2015, Obama outdid himself. Well it was not zero but your dog's monthly allowance for treats far exceeded Obama's final "gift" to seniors.

He gave the smallest non-zero increase in Social Security history—point 3. That means he gave a 0.3% increase. That amounted to just a few cents more than an average of $5.00 a month.

No pocketbook and no wallet were needed for seniors because the entire amount was gone the first second of the very first SSR payday of every month. For those receiving checks, the amount was so low on the check, the bank manager had to be called to verify an amount of a government check that was less than $5.00

Announcing a zero or 0.3 COLA to the American public is as believable as holding title to the Brooklyn Bridge. Like everybody else in America, seniors make the weekly rounds to the super market and it sure seemed that a $5.00 per month inflation boost such as what was given in Obama's last year, 2016, would not cover even the regular increase in the cost of a cheap loaf bread.

Seniors need to complain more

Why is it that regular Joe's shopping in their usual market always have a better feel for the inflation rate than the experts "calculating it." The answer is simple. We the people look at reality where the BLS analysts and coffee-breath-professor consultants do whatever they can to make the cost to the government as low as possible.

I get the feeling these stone-hearts would be happy if they could get away without paying seniors anything. The government bureaucrats and the coffee breath professors from academe would do anything, including creating new inaccurate measurements, as long as seniors would wind up with smaller increases. Ask any senior. It just isn't fair. It's time to voice a real complaint to Congress and to President Biden and pray that the elections are overturned. Let's hear it for Mike Lindell.

Chapter 4 Use Real Inflation v Government Contrivances?

The true cost of inflation is available

When you go into a market and prices have gone up, you have three choices—**1.** buy the same regardless of price because you have the money; **2.** buy less;—or **3.** leave without buying anything.

Americans have no inherent bartering system upon entering a marketplace as we find in other countries so no matter which decision we make, we survive—at least for a small while. The vendor, not the consumer, is king in America. But seniors know that for real, the government holds all the cards for seniors.

Seniors have few choices but the three annotated above. We can also try other markets after we leave the store that disappoints us. Figuring out the expensive and inexpensive stores is one of our choices and I guess, duties as a consumer. It's better for sure than no choices at all.

But, when all stores raise their prices at the same time with Congress' approval, the senior choices are minimized, especially if your income does not increase by the rate of inflation that the prices are tuned in-to.

Nobody likes being ripped off so when we check out the other stores, and their prices increase also, we know it may be an invisible hand raising all the prices but at least it is not a mechanism that we perceive as unfair. But, what if a guy writing a book such as this insists that it is very unfair for seniors. Would seniors believe me. I think not—I say regrettably.

Seniors have pride and even though they paid into SSR, many still feel a little guilty being on the take. So when the government hoses them with a minimal COLA each year, many grumble to themselves and take it on the chin. Recently many grumble and then cut back on food or get rid of a pet or so something else they should not have to do to survive.

Meanwhile the Democrats want $6 Trillion so the kind Democrats can feed illegal aliens while seniors are malnourished. It isn't fair. We just want what is our due after faithfully contributing since 1940.

What would be unfair?

IMHO, In my humble opinion, if one happens to be on a fixed income that depends on an index set based on the real cost of market goods, then what? What if the requisite adjustment to the costs does not cover the increases that we experience when we put out our real dollars to purchase real market goods? Tell me then, would our experience be worthy of a conclusion that would be a reason to feel the whole system is unfair. Yes, my friends it would be and why not?

Anybody sampling the US' faux indices such as CPI-W, would conclude the government is systematically ripping off senior citizens intentionally. And, unfortunately, they would be 100% correct. Please do yourself a favor and stop blindly trusting the government. It will put you in your grave quicker than watching their actions with skepticism. Government has violated your trust and deserve no trust anymore. Get used to it. Now, they hose seniors unabashedly and expect us all to take it. No more.

And, of course, ladies and gentlemen of the senior community, that fact would make the entire government system unfair but no government employee still will dare say a peep against the government. I mean even if they too were a senior suffering from the government's confiscation of real dollars intended for the pockets of seniors. They remain quiet and that is why the hose job happens every day for seniors.

Government is the bad guy

Thankfully to prove the potential conjecture that the government is ripping off the populace, it would help for alternative measurers to be available to evaluate the same numbers as the government's biased calculators receive as input along with coffee-breath professors from academe who are always available to put their thumbs on the scale against seniors.

Perhaps we would see the results coincide or perhaps there would be no similarities. Of course we have learned that due to BLS fraud, no honest evaluator could find coincidence. Why? Because no other indexes (those that are honest brokers of reality) have a built-in bias to stiff seniors and save the US government dollars.

Despite what appears to be *fait accompli* on putting up with government fraud against the senior community, there is good news. There are a number of better indexes available for seniors and anybody else seeking to find the true cost of living. Just knowing this, however, does not make a senior's CoLA reflect the proper inflation rate. Why? It is because the Congress would have to approve of the fact that honesty overrides chicanery and that has never happened. Congress offers its own unique brand of chicanery. Let's look at this reality a bit closer.

What would God say?

The least accurate indexes in terms of reality are those produced yearly as though they are God-like correct—the CPI-W et al. As my wife would say in terms of bringing in an accurate CoLA(cost of living adjustment) for seniors, the BLS indexes are bad, bad, bad. I need say nothing more than that but I will proceed further to complete my thoughts.

By the way CoLA does not stand for fraudulent cost of living adjustment but that is what the BLS calculators deliver to seniors. Instead of CoLA-W, it should be known as F-Cola. Make that "F" stand for whatever you want but remember, it is your own government that enables the cheating of seniors because seniors are simply so nice, the calculators and trustees of the system see gentle little sheep and know they will get away with it.

Dear seniors: Say :"No more fraud on social security," and "Give us our due reparations!"

If you check out the Walter J Williams Site—shadowstats.com, you will be surrounded by the truth on inflation. The US government's analysis of inflation factors produces little truth. You will not believe how you and all senior citizens of today, still living, have been cheated by our own government for so long. Believe it!

Walter John Williams is known by many people as John Williams. He has been the editor of the newsletter for years. He continues the publishing of this invaluable check on the reality of inflation. Thank you John.

Williams' index will show you that even in years when government says COLA is at zero, the real inflation rate is at least 5% and often as high as 10% more. That's why seniors have lost at least $15,000 or more in just the last decade. Despite the proof, the government is created to not admit this truth to the public.

Understanding all the work and the misapplied calculations that the BLS analysts do to defraud seniors is so complex, seniors feel compromised to complain. Most seniors choose not to say anything because they are not sure. Nonetheless not speaking up is the worst thing seniors can do. It sure is time for seniors to speak up against the government fraud upon their backs. It was perpetrated intentionally and once the BLS and the SSA saw that seniors would accept their numbers once, they delivered fraud every year thereafter.

To be very clear I am saying that Obama's zero CoLAs should have been at least 5% and could have been as high as 10% in those zero years. But, then again, I do not recall Obama ever saying that his major purpose was to work for the fairness or goodness of seniors.

It is my sincere hope that in this book, I prove to you that for too-many years seniors have been trampled on by government and by coffee-breathed analysts from academe. My intention is to convince enough seniors that we must all complain. Once again:

Dear seniors: Say :"No more fraud on social security," and "Give us our due reparations!"

BLS yearly produces fraudulent inflation index
See picture below:

By the way, the CPI produced by the Bureau of Labor Statistics (BLS) is as fake as measurements can go. Across the world it is known as fake news. See above.

As an aside, there is nothing bad in the picture, Jair Messias Bolsonaro is a Brazilian politician.

US Labor

There is another popular and accurate index called the Chapwood Index. I am pleased with the Shadowstats analysis and they have agreed to write a piece for this book which is included in Appendix A.

The Chapwood Index, like Shadowstats give the reader great analytics. You can look it up but I would prefer to give you all a summary of their great methodologies so you can have an easier time believing that the CPI is fake. It really is.

Shadowstats and other great sources of realistic CPI numbers are not the bad guys folks. The BLS and the SSA bureaucrats are the bad guys. Believe me while it is important that you do. The government and their friends the coffee breath professors in Academe are the perpetrators who place seniors last in the pecking order. Too bad they set the COLA rate from a fake CPI which they calculate. Life would be better without cheaters.

Please do not trust the government. Government fraudsters critique these indexes all the time while creating a CPI that does not come close to reality. Shadowstats and the Chapwood Index and others are very accurate. More importantly, they are interested in valid criticisms of their methods so they can improve to make life better for seniors.

Send your concerns to shadowstats.com for a response. They know the ripoff scheme. Register for their valuable service at a reasonable price and you too can be knowledgeable of the biggest senior ripoff since America was founded. The government cost to you, because you do not believe the truth, is much more than you can afford.

The BLS and the SSA, however, since they are government-run, want no criticism. They like laudatory fake news about their "accomplishments." These government bureaucracies do not intend to make things even a little fairer for seniors. It is not their primary mission. Their mission is to take dollars from seniors to help pay for senior-based benefits that they then give to illegal aliens. Sorry if this hurts your head but it is the truth.

The Chapwood Index is a nother good index but not as flexible as shadowstats.com. It has been designed to give a "true" inflation picture in 50 cities in the U.S.. The bureaucrats and the coffee-breath professors who calculate the government bible--CPI-W—could do this just as easily but they will not. If they did, they would be forced to give seniors an accurate cost of living adjustment that reflected the real inflation rate, not their bogus rip-off statistics.

If you think what you are getting is fair, my best advice is "Think Again." Do not trust the government. By complaining to Congress, you have a chance to change the fraudulent methodology used to calculate your CoLA.

Let's describe the Chapwood Index so you see what I mean. Remember do not trust the BLS or the SSA. Their job is to stiff you out of your real benefits increase. And, they do so very effectively each year. Many of you who had never read a Brian

Kelly Book on this topic in the past still might be finding that our own government is why so many of our friends are headed for the poorhouse and the others are preparing papers to sell their homes at 50c on the dollar. Check it out!

The Chapwood Index reflects the true cost-of-living increase in America as calculated for 50 different venues. Government does not use it because it does not short-change seniors of their true COLA. Seniors would be eating steak and caviar at least once a year if the Chapwood Index were the law of the land. Moreover, everybody would be smiling intensely…and what is wrong with that?

The Chapwood index is exactly what you and all Americans experience when you shop for anything. It represents the true cost of living increase from one year to the next. It is updated and released twice a year. It reports the unadjusted actual cost and price fluctuation of the top 500 items on which Americans spend their after-tax dollars in the 50 largest cities in the nation. It sounds fair for all Americans because it is.

It exposes why middle-class Americans — salaried workers who are given routine pay hikes and retirees who depend on annual increases in their corporate pension and Social Security payments — can't maintain their standards of living.

Plainly and simply, the Index shows that their income cannot keep up with their expenses without an accurate adjustment, and it explains why they increasingly have to turn to the government for entitlements to bail them out.

It's because salary and benefit increases are pegged to the Consumer Price Index (CPI), which for more than a century has purported to reflect the fluctuation in prices for a typical "basket of goods" in American cities — but which actually hasn't done that for more than 30 years. It started to go bad around Jimmy Carter's time and it kept getting worse. Obama gave the bad news of many zero COLAs and never expressed any remorse.

It is nice to try to fix it but half measures just won't do it.

Nice Thought but Definitely Not Enough

Not enough is definitely not enough. Robert Powell says the 2022 Social Security raise of 5.9% may be bigger than in recent years, but it's not enough to keep up with soaring inflation.

The Seniors Coalition is lobbying the House and Senate for new, guaranteed 3% CoLA Legislation to protect Social Security. But, what about the promise Roosevelt made about keeping up with real inflation?. Inflation we all know has recently surged to 10% and it is climbing while seniors are sliding. 3% does not cut it folks. Why bother. My plan is for an immediate 25% raise followed by 5% above the CPI-W rate payable every six months for the next three years.

The Seniors Coalition's legislative team may very well well-intentioned and be hard at work in both the House and Senate. Right now they are seeking an original sponsor for the Guaranteed 3% CoLA Act, originally sponsored by outgoing Congressman Eliot Engel.

Sorry folks but I do not see this as a critical piece of legislation that Seniors Coalition members have identified as critical to maintaining a comfortable life style, So inflation goes up 10% and the Coalition is asking for 3%. They are right as they have correctly suggested that as the price of goods and services continue to skyrocket, seniors struggle to keep up because of the lack of a raise in their Social Security benefits. But this legislation puts seniors behind by 7%. Who are we kidding.

They are right in suggesting that something must be done to protect Social Security for American seniors who have been forced to pay into the Social Security Trust Fund for their entire working lives. But peanuts are simply peanuts, and won't help seniors.

In the next chapter, see a great "proof" article by John Mauldin. His title tells you everything about what you ought to know his article is about:

Is the government lying to us about inflation?

Yes!

Chapter 5 Does Government Lie about Real Inflation? Yes!!!

Is Government lying to us about inflation? Yes!

BY JOHN MAULDIN; MARCH 22, 2013

Our thanks for permission to use.

In today's Outside the Box, Gary D. Halbert (my old and very dear friend and former business partner of many years) reminds us about a few significant facts concerning the Consumer Price Index (CPI) that mainstream economists and the media tend to ignore. The central question is whether the CPI is really indicative of the actual inflation rate. Not likely, says Gary, since the US Bureau of Labor Statistics (BLS), which compiles the CPI, has engaged in methodological shenanigans over the past couple decades (as has been well documented by John Williams of Shadowstats, among others).

The upshot of all their monkeying with the numbers is that the official rate of inflation may be two to four times lower than the actual rate (which is rather convenient if you're a government bureaucrat trying to hold down interest costs and Social Security payments).

[BTW, two to four times means that for every $25.00 or $50.00 you receive, it should be $100.00. Think about that @ Isn't that terrible? Screwed by our own government intentionally… This insert is from the author. That means folks that when Obama gave zero, you should have gotten 2 to 4 percent and as I recall a few of those years it was as high as 6%. That's a lot to permit yourself to not receive because of government cheating. Seniors, according to all the experts have a large payback coming. Shall we call it REPARATIONS???]

These changes are hotly debated in academic circles *[where the coffee-breath professors are prevalent.]* . There are many economists who agree with the changes and can show with their models that inflation is low. That is the currently accepted wisdom, or what passes for it. The problem is that inflation only shows up, as one person put it, in the things we actually buy.

If your main costs are food, energy, education, and healthcare (ring any bells?), then inflation is a great deal higher than 2%. Other items are actually falling in price. It comes down to the mix of items in the calculations and whether you buy into the concepts of substitution (if beef gets too expensive we buy hamburger rather than steak) and "hedonics," which says that prices of products drop over time as quality and manufacturing efficiency improve, so the calculation of inflation should take this into account.

[That, my friends is double-speak for the government having the last word, right or wrong about whether you receive a true cost of living adjustment]

Which means you can have official inflation at a low level (or even falling for certain items), while the amount you actually spend out of your very real pocket is rising! And thus the debate.

Chapter 5 Does Government Lie About Real Inflation? Yes!!!

Having refreshed us on the basic techniques of CPI massage, Gary turns to food and energy, which the BLS includes in "headline CPI" but omits from "core CPI." He points out that while headline CPI jumped an unexpected 0.7% in February, core CPI rose only 0.2%. That is, food and energy price increases accounted for more than 70% of the rise. "Not good for the economy," he notes.

And of course, this is all bad news for unwary investors, since Those who believe that inflation is only 2%, when it may be 5-8%, may be making investment decisions that are almost guaranteed to erode the purchasing power of their money over time. This is especially true with low-yielding investments such as CDs, Treasuries, etc.

Gary wraps up by taking a look at "chained CPI," which he explains as follows:

Chained CPI assumes that when prices rise, consumers will resort to entirely different products, rather than just seeking a cheaper brand. For example, if beef prices rise, chained CPI would assume that consumers might opt for chicken to save money.

The chained CPI debate is raging as we speak: I got an email from the AARP this morning, urging me to tell my Senators to say no to chained CPI being used to calculate Social Security cost-of-living adjustments (COLA) – sounds like they may vote today (Friday) on a bill to do just that.

But as Gary points out, we either calculate benefits using chained CPI – which, yes, is tough on those living on a fixed income – or we eliminate the cap on salary subject to Social Security taxation (that is, we raise taxes). As Gary says, "Either way, somebody's got to pay, and it might end up being a little [of] both."

[seniors should be out of this and should receive what Roosevelt intended, a true cost of living increase based on what seniors buy. But for too many years, the Congress, knowing this is true and knowing seniors are getting further and further behind by faulty if not downright fraudulent calculations, have permitted it to continue simply because seniors are the least likely government constituent to threaten to send a congress-person home for keeps. I hope seniors are listening.] --- End of article ---

Government Payback for Past Fraud a Must

You'll see in subsequent chapters proof that the average social security recipient has lost over $15,000 in the past decade. Since the losses for seniors are cumulative (meaning this year's increase is on top of last year's amount plus last year's COLA), technically we need to go back to the 1970's when the fraudulent calculations began with CPI-W et al.

This fraud was given to us by the Bureau of Labor Statistics on behalf of the Social Security Administration (SSA). They chose government bureaucrats and coffee breath professors from academe to systematically create arguments to reduce the inflation rate to save government dollars. The savings were intended to be raised off the backs of seniors needing to break-even year after year.

The BLS bureaucrats with their academe coffee breath professors, some smoking sweet pipe tobacco, concocted a scheme that created a fake CPI. The former CPI before the manipulators were given license to manipulate, meant the actual unadulterated rate of inflation and at the time it was legitimately called the consumer price index (CPI).

After the machinations of the bureaucratic analysts in the BLS and those under contract from academe, the CPI-W became the buzz-word for the calculation that ultimately was used with respect—as if it were legitimate—to make seniors pay dearly for their CPI machination. To repeat, in the last decade, it has cost seniors more than $15,000 on the average.

But it is a fraud. Despite its existence as a known prevarication, it is used by all government entities dealing with money and inflation. Surrogates in these areas systematically and purposefully reduce the SSR's monthly payments for senior citizens. These payments often are the major, if not the only "pension" source for a regular family. Seniors, growing up in a different time, are unaccustomed to fighting the government. To survive in these corrupt times, however, seniors will have to learn how to fight.

The truth on inflation is available outside the government

As we more than intimated in prior chapters, there are a number of reputable organizations including Walter J. Williams, aka John Williams' Shadowstats.com that have proven that the government's dishonest CPI-W misses the mark often by as much as 500%.

It produces an inflation number that is inaccurate but very favorable to the government's mission of reducing payments to SSR recipients. It is thus not a secret to our Congress that seniors are forced to move further behind each year in attempting to afford the natural increasing expenses of living.

You tell me how much this has hurt seniors. Check the foreclosures. There are no poorhouses per se anymore but more and more people today would be in the poorhouse if there was not welfare and Medicaid booster systems to help somewhat. To the heartless coffee-breath professors in academe, however, if seniors could afford to buy cat-tuna to eat themselves, they should not have to give up their homes in foreclosure. Just tighten your belts! Check it out yourself.

When you and I go to the store and something is double in price we know without checking the CPI that there is inflation. Over the years, the things we buy have been increasing by 2%; 5%; 10%; 20%; 50%; and even higher and new things with larger continual increases have been added to the senior citizens' burden.

Can seniors afford life with a crooked CoLA?

It may not be a gut punch that gives seniors a real black eye. However, the government hurts seniors in the worst possible place—their ability to be able to afford to live.

Can you believe that such excluded items from the BLS list include health insurance, medical expenses, gasoline, car expenses, and huge property taxes, other taxes and fees as well as new but deemed necessary items.

Seniors get zero while paying for others such as the welfare class, government employees, and illegal aliens. For example, in my home town, every year that Obama denied seniors any COLA, city employees actually got a 3% pay raise. Their raise of course was paid for by local tax increases paid by seniors.

Why should seniors be expected to choose between eating, foreclosure, eating their pet cat, growing goldfish for food, or going to jail?. Is this not America?

Soon, you will see how quickly my "generous" $24.00 per month total increase (COLA) for 2020 was gone. It was a sin and it is the product of blatant government corruption. Let me preview it by saying that when I looked at my least expensive health item, pharmacy, the entire COLA of $24.00 per month was consumed by this one item.

Then, of course, my wife and I as well as your wives and you, with nothing left from the COLA, were forced to absorb all of the other price increases from bread to milk to meat, with the magical 1.6% bogus COLA for SSR. But, there was nothing left from the COLA as Pharma had eaten it all. .

It was totally inadequate. Yet, not only did seniors get stiffed but, unlike a veteran in the VA, there was no agency to whom to complain? Who ya gonna call? Even Ghost Busters could not answer because they are only in movies. So, I got the answer: "Nobody!" Not even Ghost Busters! Think about it. Call nobody. Crawl into a corner so that your own body heat will not be lost. Take some pillows with you. The BLS and the SSA have done seniors no favors.

Which agency represents seniors' needs and handles their legitimate gripes?

Actually, there is no such agency!

There is no government agency that looks after the senior population as does the VA for veterans. seniors respect veterans and are pleased the veterans under Trump now have a legitimate agency helping them. No senior would ever deny veterans any of their well-earned gains.

I already gave the answer of "nobody." .Which government agency is charged with making sure seniors get a fair shake out of life. I am thankful that we finally have a better-run Veterans administration, which until President Trump said, *"stop the crap,"* when he ruled the roost, recently, had previously been letting the Vets down. We all know now that the Vets are covered by the Trump decree. We are all very happy that our past president took this posture for Vets. Many seniors are long-term Vets.

Unfortunately, as I write this new book about the government exploitation of seniors, there is no *seniors administration* that I can find that would make it as easy for any president so inclined to make a proclamation that would benefit seniors and have it implemented as swiftly as Trump's VA proclamation helped the veterans.

Nobody, even seniors who are wanting, would ever consider denying the veterans their legitimate claims to benefits. In fact, I would suggest that seniors more than any other group of Americans root for the veterans because nobody knows as much as seniors about how great the veterans have been in making life better for all Americans.

Many seniors are current or past soldiers and vice versa. Seniors do not want to compete with soldiers. That is for sure. Soldiers assure democracy and seniors become soldiers in their early lives.

Funny about how we all age—almost all my buddies today are senior citizens and I love them all. I do not care whether they are liberal or conservative. They are my buddies. All seniors of which I am aware respect all soldiers and are very thankful for their hard work in defense of our country.

Just because there is no agency for seniors today, does not mean that former President Trump or President Joe Biden cannot effect any positive change that he is convinced must be made for seniors. Trump was a good president and a good man and certainly did not want to short-change seniors and make their lives difficult. Joe Biden doesn't seem to care.

I hope somebody will tell the President about this book being written to help seniors. I hope that after reading this book that President Biden will have an idea of the best solutions for seniors for the future.

Chapter 6 It's Time for "The Seniors Administration."

Senior's advocates could influence govt decision makers.

I for one believe that when an agency is created for seniors, life will get better. If the Agency broadcasted the plight of today's senior citizens, they would also insist that the Congress create a great Seniors Administration (SA) that would be comparable in quality with the Veterans' Administration (VA) without all of the special funding needs.

Senior funding today comes from the people who contribute or have contributed to the FICA payroll deduction for most of their lives. It is administered by the Social Security Administration (SSA) and the COLA is calculated and also diminished by the Bureau of Labor Statistics (BLS).

A dedicated Senior Administration (SA) agency would measure among other major plusses for seniors. It would stop a negligent Congress from continuing to stiff seniors from reasonable increases to stay even with inflation.

Who would not love to see the days of home foreclosures and life style minimization come to an end abruptly. Just because seniors are older, does not mean we do not deserve a happy life.

Before President Donald Trump solved the VA issues by making veterans a national priority, things were not so good. Then, the President set the Veterans Administration on a course to make life right for veterans. Despite solid military traditions, life was not so good for the many who had given so much for our country.

Unlike many presidents before him, Donald Trump used his smarts and his raw determination and he fixed the problem for veterans. It is worthy of note to repeat that this was after many presidents before him had failed. I know that a president with the right focus can do the same thing with the Seniors Administration (SA).

One of those sacred traditions in the military is *leave no one behind on the battlefield*. But many injured veterans had begun to believe their country had left them behind at home, once they were out of uniform and in need of help. That help was supposed to come from the Department of Veterans Affairs and the financial compensation it gave to veterans who had been disabled by their military service. Veterans all of a sudden, it seemed, had it tough getting a timely VA appointment. The former President changed that, making it much better for all veterans.

It was one of his first priorities in June 2017, when President Donald Trump signed a landmark law on veterans' health care after months of tense negotiations. At the ceremony in the Rose Garden, Trump said the bill would deliver on his campaign promise to let veterans see private doctors instead of using the Department of Veterans Affairs' government-run health service: "I'm going to sign legislation that will make veterans' choice permanent," he said.

That moment left no doubt that the Trump administration was and still is determined to use the new law to expand the private sector's role in veterans' health care. No more long lines at the VA hospital. This change for veterans is monumental. Trump is a big difference maker for veterans.

Any president who cares about seniors can play as important a role in the problems that seniors are having in getting a fair shake from the government. A Politico headline saw this as the new mantra for Democrats in their disdain for seniors:

"Democrats to seniors: *Drop Dead.*"

As noted previously, even though the military's slogan for years has been *leave no one behind on the battlefield*, before Donald Trump vowed to solve the problem at the VA, far too many veterans had begun to believe their country had left them behind at home, once they were out of uniform and in need of help.

The president took the right action and things are now much better in terms of the Veterans Administration. With Trump full-time on the job, few Vets today have to remember this was their old motto:

"Delay, Deny and Hope That I Die."

Before Trump, at the VA, this was reality!

Few can deny that with the callous treatment seniors receive from the same government, they have been left behind. It has been a long time since seniors got a fair shake. It was back at least when the CPI-W was instituted during the recession of 1973-1975. seniors have been left behind and in the woods. Those past their prime today need a real slogan very much like the battlefield slogan of the veterans to help guide the care that is to be given to America's greatest generation and those who qualify for SSR.

Most Americans today are well aware that the "Greatest Generation" refers to those Americans, all of whom are now seniors. They were born in the 1900s through the 1920s. The Greatest Generation members all lived through the Great Depression and many of them fought in World War II. The Greatest Generation members also tend to be the parents of the Baby Boomer generation. Some historians stretch the greatest generation well through the 1940's and even into the 1950's to respect the role today's elderly had in saving America during World War II.

Stretching the Greatest Generation to Other Demographics

Categorizing the generations is an inexact notion depending on who is marking off the years. Generally speaking, the Greatest Generation are the parents of the "Baby Boomers" and are the children of the "Lost Generation" (those who grew up during or came of age during World War I). They preceded what is known as the "Silent Generation," a cohort born between the mid-1920s to the early-to-mid 1940s, which some stretch through the 1950's.

The grandchildren of the Greatest Generation therefore are members of Generation X, , Generation Y, and the Millennials. For our purposes the following chart works well for this book:

The Generations

Greatest / Silent Generation	**1910-1945**
Baby Boomers	**1946-1964**
Generation X	**1965-1979**
Millennials/ Generation Y	**1980-1984**

The senior citizen designation for "old farts" like me is not a legal term but is most often used for Americans over age 49. Since normal social security payments can begin at age 62, those above this age are most often known as senior citizens or seniors. If you are not yet 62, you may still be eligible for social security if you are disabled. I know, like many of the seniors reading this book, I would prefer to be fully functional rather than disabled and having to wait a few years for benefits. Nobody denies the disabled their due.

Here is the Social Security Administration's definition of disability: You are entitled to receive Social Security disability

(SSDI) or Supplemental Security Income (SSI) benefits when you are no longer able to perform a "substantial" amount of work as the result of a physical or mental impairment that is expected to last at least 12 months, or possibly result in death. To Social Security, a substantial amount of work, called "substantial gainful activity," is making $1,220 or more per month, before taxes (or $2,040 per month for people who are blind, in 2019).

Even though many collecting SSR do not know this, it is possible for someone who has never worked a day to obtain disability benefits under a program called SSI or "Supplemental Security Income." Fortunately, people who become disabled but have never worked are covered under the SSI program if they do not qualify for Social Security Disability. Since these folks did not contribute, there is some resentment, yet, nobody would like to trade their benefits for anybody else's disability.

Raises come to all SSR and disability recipients but they are not intended to be raises. They are intended to be break-even adjustments so that the ravages of inflation do not put all seniors and the disabled in the proverbial poorhouse.

Cost of Living Adjustments

All SS Recipients get an automatic cost-of-living increase when they are on disability or when they are simply collecting their due. recompense. A cost-of-living adjustment (COLA) is available to everyone who receives benefits from a Social Security program, including Social Security Disability Insurance (SSDI), Supplemental Security Income (SSI), and Social Security Retirement (SSR).

The issues regarding the COLA as discussed in this book are germane for all recipients of Social Security benefits, not just for those collecting retirement. The Social Security Administration (SSA) administers SSDI.

42 What About Seniors?

Some 8.5 million people receive disabled-worker benefits from Social Security. Payments also go to some of their family members: 117,000 spouses and 1.5 million children.

More than 8 million people—including 1.2 million children with disabilities—rely on SSI to meet their basic needs. Monthly benefits average just $541. The Social Security Administration runs SSI

Is Social Security Bad News?

Social Security is tremendous. It is a life-saving government program—probably the gest government program there ever was. It is without a doubt—a wonderful program. Without it, many senior citizens would not have been and still would not be able to survive.

In my research for this book, I could not find statistics for the years that life was lengthened for those seniors who were collecting SSR benefits versus the very same seniors if they were not able to collect the benefits (adjusted for inflation) of their contributions.

If I were to estimate with no supporting data, my guess would be that 20% of all seniors collecting benefits would have died much sooner without the major benefits provided by the SSR system.

My rough estimate would be that seniors on SSR would last at least five years longer than those not on such benefits. That would mean 20% (X 60 million on SSR==12 million) of all beneficiaries gained 5 years onto their natural lives.

That would mean that 12 million people would have lived five years longer. So, we can say that every five years, over 60 million people have lived five years longer. That is a major benefit for Social Security. Moreover, all of these beneficiaries paid in something so this is not welfare. SSR is a great system.

Much of this book is about the COLA (Cost of Living Adjustment). Bureaucrats and coffee-breath professors in academe, think COLA should be ACOLA (*Almost cost of living adjustments*).

COLA for SSR and SSDI and SSI is designed to keep senior benefits steady (constant) regardless of inflation. The reason this is important today more than in the past is that the work of the BLS in shortchanging the COLA has taken its toll on the ability for seniors to survive in life.

By not keeping the market basket constant, the BLS exerts a cumulative negative effect on the ability of seniors to make ends meet. Inflation was understated so that seniors could not maintain their normal lives with the same relative ability to afford living as time was moving on.

As great a system that the contributory pension scheme of Social Security provided over the years, its goodness was diminished by BLS Bureaucrats and coffee-breath professors who had forgotten that the numbers they produced as a "CPI," affected real people who did not know they had signed up for a charade.

The real people counted on a 1940 dollar being adjusted each year by a true consumer price index, not a cheating imitation concocted by glory seeking bureaucrats looking for kudos by stiffing seniors.

President Roosevelt's intention for SSR was not to diminish the dollar's purchasing power of seniors as inflation hit the economy each year over time. His idea was to lift the dollar up so that it had what could be called a constant value for all and its value could be counted on even as it differed from the face value. Its value was not supposed to be decreased over the years. The purpose of Social Security was always for the elderly to retire with dignity. Stealing what keeps seniors breaking even every year shortchanges that dignity.

Unfortunately, because of the BLS bureaucrats and the coffee-breathed professors in academe, the temptation for the bureaucrats to give money back to the US treasury has ruled the day. There is no concern for dignity of any kind and government cheating is permitted or by now people would be in jail. The BLS found that the true COLA could easily be stolen from seniors. This was far too great a temptation for these government employees and contractors to give a flat "no!" to the scheme. They chose to be dishonest to please their higher-ups.

So, systematically seniors have been denied the full breakeven calculations. Instead without revealing the net effect of their charade, the government analysts and contractors have reported the CPI as being far less than it really was—as if it were a true measure of inflation. Each year, the reality of their work product takes real money right out of the wallets of seniors.

This would have been an innocuous notion if the jerrymandered numbers were not used to fool senior Americans who required a fair and accurate consumer price index (CPI). Instead, what seniors got and still get is a Kentucky-windage estimate that serves their low-life purposes for reducing the adjustment seniors receive.

There is no question that social security itself from Roosevelt onward, even with the cheating, extends the lives of seniors. However, the bureaucrats have made it very difficult to make ends meet for seniors by not treating the COLA fairly. It was not supposed to be this way. To give a perspective, please check out the chart on the following page.

Like the Veterans forced to cry out because for years at the poorly run VA Hospital system, they had been left behind, seniors suffer similar abuse. Where ineptitude seemed part of the VA's problem, seniors are actually cheated by the government intentionally. Think about that sentence for a while. Chew on it.

With major publications characterizing a major political party's best suggestion for seniors as "Drop Dead," it is clear that Democrat Party respect for what seniors deserve has dropped to an all-time low in recent times. Nobody who "drops dead" has to be paid by the Social Security system. Is that what this is?

Life Expectancy for Social Security

Year Cohort Turned 65	Percentage of Population Surviving from Age 21 to Age 65		Average Remaining Life Expectancy for Those Surviving to Age 65	
	Male	Female	Male	Female
1940	53.9	60.6	12.7	14.7
1950	56.2	65.5	13.1	16.2
1960	60.1	71.3	13.2	17.4
1970	63.7	76.9	13.8	18.6
1980	67.8	80.9	14.6	19.1
1990	72.3	83.6	15.3	19.6

Additionally, no oversight government agency is charged to make sure that seniors are being treated properly by the government. The Department of Veterans Affairs does that job for veterans and even with them, the VA system became a sham until Trump fixed it. There is no agency making sure that Seniors are not being mistreated by the government. I would say having the Bureau of Labor Statistics (BLS) steal money that with a little honesty would be going into the pockets of seniors, is a prosecutable crime. Too bad seniors get "screwed" and nobody cares.

Clearly times have changed and not for the good. Let me say this again. There is no group inside or outside of government whose mission it is to assure that senior citizens on Social Security are not left behind. Stealing from seniors with impunity would be one way to prove to seniors that they are indeed left behind.

It is time for a real slogan for seniors that is loaded with respect and dignity for the greatest generation and generations that will surely follow. "Drop Dead" is not acceptable. My suggestion is simple but appropriate:

"Every senior's life is worthwhile—no exceptions"

Americans know if this notion were brought to the attention of a good President, with all the seniors of today teetering at the poverty border, it would become his national priority. It is up to us all to help seniors get noticed by our President and our Congress.

It was Abraham Lincoln who said the purpose of the VA was to "care for him who shall have borne the battle." But the wars in Iraq and Afghanistan pushed the VA further behind in that mission, and on the way to President Trump, there were a million veterans waiting for the VA to handle their disability claims.

As we noted previously, that had led some veterans to find solace by latching onto another motto that had made the rounds for how the VA had been operating: "Delay, Deny and Hope That I Die." Thanks to President Trump, things have changed for Veterans.

Would it not be nice if seniors had a day and if seniors had their own Seniors Administration run by a gentleman as capable and compassionate as former US Secretary of Veterans Anthony Joseph Principi. Now that Trump has the Veterans Administration running smooth like it is part of the military again, seniors know that such an organization for seniors would be very welcome. As you read this nice message from Secretary Principi, think about just how wonderful such an organization would be to serve seniors.

Veterans Affairs reform became reality under President Trump

The facts in this section were researched and presented by Anthony Principi, Opinion Contributor for The Hill on 11/11/19 10:00 AM EST (Veterans Day). Your author is thankful to the great insights and prose provided by Mr. Principi. Anthony Joseph Principi was born April 16, 1944. He served as the fourth United States Secretary of Veterans Affairs.

He was appointed by President George W. Bush on January 23, 2001, and he resigned on January 26, 2005. Princip knows the VA

System and he knows the Trump administration changes that have made it much better.

The latest reforms at the Department of Veterans Affairs under the Trump administration give me a lot of hope on this Veterans Day. As a veteran myself, I recognize that we must do more than honor the sacrifices and achievements of those who have answered the call of duty. It is about remembering our own duty as a society to ensure veterans are not left to fend for themselves with the challenges and issues service can bring.

I served during the Vietnam War, a conflict that put tremendous strain on servicemen and women and their families. Then 18 years of sustained conflict since 9/11 resulted in even more of the same stresses. Under that pressure, the safeguards we had in place to protect veterans faltered. By the final years of the Obama administration, the situation had blossomed into a full blown crisis, with veterans reportedly dying on waiting lists.

During the 2016 campaign, Donald Trump made correcting this problem one of his top priorities, and he has not relented on that objective since taking office. To that end, he has done everything in his power to wind down the seemingly endless wars of the last two administrations and avoid entangling our troops in anymore bloody overseas conflicts.

President Trump has been adamant that Veterans Affairs establish the key programs to care for both the physical and psychological wounds of our returning service members. Through taking executive action and signing bipartisan reforms into law, he has time and again demonstrated his own commitment to delivering the reforms our veterans deserve. He has also made sure the government provides them adequate resources.

The budget allocation was a record $201 billion for Veterans Affairs this year, and the budget request for next year calls for raising that figure to $220 billion. Some of that money will go toward attracting medical and management talent to Veterans Affairs that was lacking in certain areas, a task furthered by the Veterans Affairs Choice and Quality Employment Act. The Trump administration has also taken crucial steps to improve the prospects of future veterans. The National Defense Authorization Act this year has raised military salaries by 2.6 percent, the most in nine years.

Money is not everything, though, which is why President Trump has also worked with lawmakers to reform how Veterans Affairs works and will continue to ensure that dollars are spent wisely for our veterans and their families. To that end, he signed the Veteran Appeals Improvement and Modernization Act, the Veterans Affairs Accountability and Whistleblower Protection Act, and the Mission Act, all designed to create flexible new treatment options while building a culture of accountability. The Mission Act notably allows veterans to use benefits at private medical facilities if their local Veterans Affairs hospital is unable to fully meet their needs.

On his own authority, President Trump has signed executive orders to improve treatment at Veterans Affairs. Understanding that suicide and mental health issues are very often as devastating as any physical injury incurred in the service, President Trump signed two executive orders specifically addressing suicide among veterans, which has ballooned to tragic levels. Veterans who live far from traditional federal hospitals can take advantage of new telehealth options to connect with doctors and therapists, including mental health professionals, from their homes.

The White House also launched an official hotline two years ago to help veterans navigate the complexities of the Department of Veterans Affairs. Since then, the hotline, primarily staffed by veterans and direct family members of veterans, has fielded more than a quarter million calls from veterans and resolved an impressive 94 percent of its cases. Our duty to our veterans is eternal. This year's and every future Veterans Day, Americans can be proud that our commander in chief is honoring our national promise to them.

Administration on Aging

The closest thing to a VA for senior citizens is known as *The Administration on Aging (TAA)*. It is a nice idea but it simply is not enough. No cigars go for this agency but it is better than nothing.

You can tell the difference in scope of various government programs by looking at their respective budgets. It also gives an idea how far a program such as the seniors administration (SA) would have to go before it began to make a dent in the issues with the elderly population.

With a $2 Billion budget, The Administration on Aging (TAA) allocation is not chump change but compared to over $200 Billion for the VA, you can see that the purpose of the TAA is light advocacy for the aging whereas the VA is a substantive solution to Veterans' issues.

Most of us already know the purpose and the reach of the VA system. It is a real difference maker for veterans, Thank God it now works. The TAA as an agency to help seniors is 1/100 the size of the VA. Its mission currently is to work to keep other government organizations aware of the issues that influence seniors so that legislation affecting the senior population keeps their needs and issues top of mind, and they provide grants to various other organizations that provide direct services and education to seniors

That is a fine mission but there is a problem. Most seniors know nothing about the agency. If its purpose were as a simple advocacy group to stop other government agencies from ripping off seniors by reducing the COLA, the Administration on Aging would be much more welcome by seniors. But nobody, of whom I am aware, knows what it is or does.

Consider this $2Billion dollars bureaucracy about which its principal client—all the seniors in America, are mostly unaware. This tells the whole story. The agency is obviously not impacting seniors in any meaningful way. I am seventy-one years old. This means I have been a senior about ten years and I have never heard of this agency.

What would give it purpose is if its mission were to satisfy the needs of seniors by being an advocate for legislation as well as a conduit for the President to understand better the problems seniors face. I have yet to hear President Trump speak once about the COLA rip-off, which costs seniors as much as $15,000 in one decade and then since it is cumulative, it costs more as time goes by.

We all know how President Trump enjoyed being able to help veterans. President Biden speaks little about seniors. We should be sure that any president would likewise help seniors if he were tuned into this nasty trick pulled off by government.

There are 64 million Americans collecting social security. Putting a smile on that many people is something I am sure the president would enjoy. There are about 20 million veterans. Not all veterans are currently collecting benefits but the President has been their personal advocate and they know it.

Seniors understand the roles of the Bureau of Labor Statistics (BLS) and the Social Security Administration (SSA) in setting the COLA and sending out the monthly payments and keeping the accounting books accurate. However, those of us who look at these agencies in more depth know enough about them to see them as the misers they are.

SSA has done nothing to solve the big senior rip-off of which they are aware and the BLS, comprised of green eye shade bureaucrats, are the very perpetrators who commit the major theft against seniors. BLS provides the fraudulent cost of living increase to seniors once a year. The more seniors know about BLS the more BLS is despised.

I would think that with funding of substantially less than one $Billion per year, for a brand new Seniors Administration, the president could light up the faces of almost 65 million seniors. I know I would like to see a US President get to work and then take the kudos for this initiative. President Trump can create an army of seniors' advocates even if he is not president now. The Seniors Administration (SA) needs only one important mission--IMHO.

The mission would be very simple. The BLS and the SSA have been joined together at the hip in an unholy alliance against seniors for far too many years to count. They create a purposefully inaccurate cost of living estimate that need not be an estimate. Estimates are not needed. All that must be done is determine a real cost of living using the same old market basket methodology from way back. That idea worked well long before the government's exotic calculators began to stiff seniors.

No more estimates. Anything post-facto should be historical fact— not a possibility. The inflation rate is the inflation rate. Period. All Americans know the difference in the cost of living from the market basket right before the Carter years to the BLS market basket of today. Putting elements that can only hurt seniors into the basket is a fraud. It's time for the government to admit their malfeasance and begin to do it right. Hire the Shadowstats gang and it would not cost a ton to implement.

The time is over for government bureaucrats and academe rip-off artists balancing the budget on the backs of seniors. That is exactly what the their very clever, but fraudulent CPI-W calculation produces They know that nobody, for more than a few years, can live on a number that does not even approximate the true cost of living.

Seniors have been punished by government for far too long. Just like President Trump gave the Veterans their due, if a president is given the facts on seniors, he would never accept that seniors need to barely survive on subsistence living. Conditions for seniors are poor and getting worse, not better. In Seminole Country Florida, the fastest growing segment of homeless are among the elderly. Ask yourself how it must feel being 85 and homeless? Seniors are not prepared to look for handouts. They did not grow up that way. They want only the amount due when the real cost of living is taken into consideration, not BLS estimates full of fraud.

For too many seniors, the contrived, fraudulent CPI-W from BLS and administered by SSA, has already put enough seniors in the grave as paupers. The Congress can find the time to initiate a program for seniors that is as fair as the VA program but far less expensive and expansive. . Creating the Seniors Administration (SA) is a great start.

Seniors search for fairness

Seniors are not greedy people as presented by the Democrats and today's dishonest senior-hating media. Anybody who has had over $15,000 stolen from them by government's intentional miscalculations over a decade, would naturally be upset. Seniors are simply looking for an honest cost of living number, not a fake number put together by government hacks and coffee breath professors in academe.

Even our esteemed Congress has known the solution for many years; yet they have chosen to do nothing. Congress has known that seniors have been in great stress and still they have enacted no solution. For their failure to do their jobs, seniors need to mildly revolt , take their names, and send this entire Congress packing.

Seniors want to keep their ability to spend SSR at the same level each year. Nobody has ever said our elderly are not entitled to an ice cream cone every now and then. But without announcing the truth, the government has teams of experts and lawyers fighting fairness every year to stiff seniors from receiving their due.

Your mother and grand-mother are seniors. Perhaps like me, you too are a senior. You know seniors are kind and loving. In fact, if seniors paid more attention to the acts of Congress, the real bad guys, these rogues would have been out of office a long time ago.

Seniors are not asking the government for more than "same." From the poor / fraudulent treatment they have been given by analysts with a mission, they have an inherent right not be forced into the poor-house to accept "less" than their due.

Unlike the Congressional elites, senior citizens need and therefore, look forward for a monthly check from SSR that honestly reflects reality. SSR COLAs are not supposed to take money from seniors and ultimately bankrupt seniors. Instead the dollar payments to seniors are to be constant when their inflationary value is taken into consideration.

If the cost of living is $1.00, seniors should receive $1.00 not $.79 because somebody in government figured they could snooker seniors into accepting lower than actual COLAs. Seniors from year to year by law are supposed to receive all the costs that are actually paid to live from year to year and not a dime more. No senior nor Franklin Roosevelt, the Father of SSR, even said that should not include the costs for health care.

For a country that sent a man to the moon over 50 years ago in 1969, one would think that by now it ought to be pretty easy for the United States to figure out the right method. Don't you think? Why, unless the government is purposely defrauding seniors, has the solution not yet been expounded and adopted by Congress and endorsed by the President?

A proper conclusion is that government has been operating against the people since the Jimmy Carter Administration in the 1970's. Isn't that long enough. It got worse in 1983. Is it not time for President Trump, like he solved the VA crisis. To solve the senior crisis.

Amen!

Chapter 7 How Would a Seniors Administration (SA) Help Seniors?

seniors looking for help to out-think a government CABAL

The chapter title unfortunately tells too much. Why should seniors need protection against the US government? And, why would anybody think that the US government would be the best vehicle to provide such support?

The answer to the second question is the most important. We have seen recently when major advocacy agencies such as the VA are reengaged, they do a fine job. Seniors would like a model agency built somewhat like the VA in its determination to do right by seniors to lead an effort to make things as they should be for the elderly community in America. I am especially talking about those seniors on social security as well as citizens on SSI and SSDI, who are subject today to the whims of a rogue agency, the BLS, comprised of uncaring bureaucrats and coffee-breath professors from academe.

The answer to the first question is because the Bureau of Labor Statistics (BLS) on behalf of the Social Security Administration has found that with no oversight such as from a watchdog seniors administration, they have been able to run roughshod over the elderly with impunity. The major victims have been those collecting social security benefits. Since the BLS is a government agency and since they have been committing the crime of theft from seniors for over 36 years, they must be stopped. After so many years, it is clear, they do not plan to stop themselves.

In most cases, I would be the first to say that the government is on the side of the citizens. But, in budgetary matters in which at least theoretically, every dime counts; it is clear that we cannot expect government employees to act differently than the way they perceive their mission. And, so the citizens need oversight so that we do not get government of, for, and by the government as opposed to of, for, and by the people.

In simple terms, seniors have many sources of proof for what is happening in practice with the BLS. There is proof. For example when seniors are entitled to two, the government says one is more than enough. Instead of receiving the proper entitlement of two dollars, for example, you receive one. Shadowstats and the Chapwood Index and others have proven the culpability of the BLS in this open fraud upon seniors.

How long would it be for the government to not be on your friend's list if you were really convinced that what I just said were true? And, of course it is true. I regret to say this, folks—especially to seniors who believe government is good. "Today, especially for seniors, government is not your best friend." Not even close.

If you put two of something in a government account, expecting three today, you would be lucky to find one. Moreover, you will get no apology. Government provides no accountability for its perpetrations. Seniors are unlucky perhaps that we are at the bottom of the Democrat list of good guys, and the media unapologetically worships the Democrats. What chance do seniors have to get a fair shake? None with today's stacked deck! That's why the Senior Administration is needed ASAP.

Start your recovery process by believing all the facts that are stacked against your success and then work to mitigate those who are on the attacking side. They normally have a big "D" on their sweatshirts. Check it out!

Government bureaucrats from the BLS and the coffee-breath professors with big calculators needed to sustain their huge consulting contracts use smart play as defined by W.C. Fields to separate seniors from an honest cost of living adjustment. Bureaucrats and consultants need a patsy to have their stings work on regular joe's. Most seniors are over trusting and are thus easy prey when government is ready to pounce and take rather than analyze and help. W.C. Fields taught Democrats well:

"You can't cheat an honest man; never give a sucker an even break, or smarten up a chump." Government bureaucrats and coffee breath professors are in the game for their own gain and they don't give one hoot about how their decisions affect you or other seniors.

And, so, folks, to avoid being a sucker, your job is to recognize this and root for yourself rather than the government entities that claim to have your back. Lobby Congress for a Seniors Administration. The government agencies supporting your pension do not have your back. In fact, with regard to Social Security benefits, government is clearly on the opposite side. Get used to it. They will not admit it; but it is how it is.

If the protein in cat tuna equals the protein in steak, does it matter which you eat? In their analyses, why would government workers even consider such questions—but they do. If they find out that you really like cat tuna, will they raise its price in the BLS stats to that of Filet Mignon? Would any government official suggest seniors should eat dog food?

Years ago, I would have answered differently. However, looking at the COLA results for seniors and the government explanations over the last thirty or more years, it is clear that the people in the BLS and their cohorts in academe—you know who I mean—the coffee breath professors on lucrative contracts--have one and only one mission, and it has nothing to do with being fair to senior citizens.

It is to reduce the cost of seniors to the federal budget To do this, they must figure out legitimate-looking, yet illegitimate ways to stiff seniors of their proper COLA. Both the bureaucrats and the coffee-breathers feel no need to check the original SSR contracts so their decrees simply minimize the rights of seniors to break-even year-to-year. With no oversight from a Seniors Administration to stop them, their "innovations" get more outrageous each year. Check out the new Chained CPI, a contrived way to reduce COLA even further. Make sure you always say "no" to the Chained-CPI no matter who is proposing it.

A Seniors Administration is vital. Despite the fact that compared to consumers who ate steak in 1973; Hamburg in 1984; tuna in 2000; and cat tuna in 2012, seniors have been losing net worth. No seniors today are expecting or even asking the BLS to turn the clocks back to the filet mignon days instead of cat food tuna, which is the BLS protein of choice in 2021 But, folks, even without filet mignon, respect for seniors can and should be lots better than it is.

Who would have ever determined that cat tuna would evolve into becoming the correct protein substitute for steak ? Whoever dreamed that up the first time should be identified post haste and post facto, and be fired.

Democrats speak out of both sides of their mouths and Republicans are interested in saving government budget dollars to solidify Social Security funding (code word for reducing) on the backs of elderly people. Meanwhile seniors are losing their homes and having trouble making ends meet. With Seniors in just about every family, this is a terrible trick being played on the entire country by a deceitful government.

Democrats suggest ways to increase benefits and then out of the other side of their mouth, they send out their media hacks like

Samuelson from the Washington Post who wrote a column recently titled: "Don't expand Social Security. Our elderly are mostly fine." Glad you think so Mr. Samuelson. How much has government fake calculations on the CPI cost you recently? However much it is; it is too much.

His talking points net out to his idea that expanding Social Security is mostly a political bribe that comes at the expense of other programs and workers, who must pay the resulting taxes. Seems like Samuelson wants seniors to demand that their benefits get cut. Fat chance. Seniors may be getting old but they are not nuts.

How would the Seniors Administration Function?

Government likes to set up agencies that purportedly are there to help people. My proposal in these two chapters is to create one of those agencies and call it the *Seniors Administration (SA)*. The role of this agency would be simple—to prevent other government agencies such as the Social Security Administration (SSA) and the Bureau of Labor Statistics BLS from pillaging and defrauding seniors.

How would this be done? The SA would not be a full-service agency like the VA. It would simply be a watchdog to make sure they SSA and the BLS can never go south again on the American people.

A separate group from the current BLS CPI-team needs to be established who. Their job would be to contract with an outside group such as the Shadowstats Group and the Chapwood Group where the true inflation rate would be calculated as part of their normal business. From these outside groups, the true inflation rate would be determined and the Seniors Administration would make sure that it is correct before passing it on to the BLS to be announced to the public.

Since the government owes seniors over $2.5 trillion, most of that amount will be paid back. How? It will be according to the Payback Plan and the payback program will be finished in three years as follows:

Beginning in 2020, instead of the normal CPI-W that has been the method for 36 years, instead for a three year period, seniors will receive a 10% COLA twice a year. Ten percent will be distributed in January and ten percent will be distributed in July. This will have the effect of a 20% increase per year for seniors but since it will be cumulative every six months (Bases on the SSR payment at the time), the overall effect each year will be somewhat more than 20% in total. After the 6th payment, seniors will begin to receive an amount calculated by the real inflation rate once a year as their annual COLA

"Safeguard against the hazards and vicissitudes of life"

Roosevelt never suggested that seniors be stiffed if the government decided it did not want to keep the dollars constant. To be sure, Roosevelt's proposition on June 8, 1934, "promised a plan for social insurance as a safeguard "against the hazards and vicissitudes of life." Today, I regret the hazards and vicissitudes have come mostly from the BLS and SSA – agencies of the government itself. SSR recipients need to be paid back for all their losses according to the prescription announced above.

Can the dead corpses of seniors help the government make its bottom-line numbers?. Is there any group of which any of us are aware that represents senior citizens in the same fashion as the Vets are represented and supported by the VA?

Review New Agency: Seniors Administration

Causes such as this make me dream about helping more and more Americans. There is no question that the best way to achieve the fairness goal of seniors is to create this brand new advocacy group called the "SA." Like the VA is the *Veterans Administration*, the SA would become the *Seniors Administration*.

This would be a group that is not held back by Congress and the Academe. The purpose would be to assure the longevity of the senior contingent in America. Most seniors would consider that a big, positive change.

The worst thing that the constant decrease in yearly SSR benefits has done to seniors is produce a "what's the use" attitude. Many seniors have grown despondent watching others in their plights lose their homes because they had to deal with ever increasing taxes which were not factored into their SSR raises. When you can't eat; eventually you die.

Many seniors trusted President Obama to do the right thing for seniors, yet he came out as a president who did not stick up for the elderly. The facts suggest that seniors did not matter to the prior President or he would have acted. In fact, Obama was the zero-man. He was the first president to give a zero percent increase or an almost zero percent increase. Worse than that he did it in four of his eight years as president. Meanwhile market prices were inflating through the roof.

Seniors should be given some respect by their position in life's hierarchy.

It is intuitive that young people are not hatched from eggs. Yet, too many millennials choose to consider seniors as consumers who consume and produce nothing valuable for society. They forget that without the tender, loving care of seniors in their productive years, millennials could not and thus would not exist.

All young people in America have been brought forth from seniors in one way or another. Just like all people in American society have been permitted to live because of the bravery of soldiers who receive support from the VA.

Additionally, all soldiers were raised by the good will of a set of parents who today are more than likely seniors. How could our America forget that?

Congress has demonstrated that it cares little about seniors. Despite their history of being abused by the annual BLS COLA, seniors remain too kind-hearted. History has proven that seniors would reelect a corrupt Congress without knowing their real records. Seniors have a tough time believing their precious government would intentionally harm them.

Mitchell Langbert, an associate professor of business management at Brooklyn College, recently reviewed the party affiliations of 8,688 tenure-track, Ph.D.-holding professors at 51 of the top 60 liberal arts colleges listed in U.S. News and World Report's 2017 rankings.

FYI, Business professors are where academe sometimes squeezes in one or two Republicans because most Democrats do not understand business. As you might suspect, exceptional talent in writing poetry does not help when tackling accounting and finance issues.

Nearly 60 percent of all faculty members were registered as either a Republican or a Democrat, and of that sample, there were 10.4 times as many Democrats as Republicans. It is what it is. So, it is the Democrats in Academe, lacking business experience, who are most often the ones setting the consumer price index in cahoots with Democrat bureaucrats from the government.

For far too many years, government and academe, especially Dems have openly conspired to stiff seniors by obtuse calculations which logic would never assert as correct. The results are devastating to seniors as these academe and government dunderheads set the "inflation rate" using their own machinated Kentucky windage formula.

By design, this causes seniors to struggle more and more to make ends meet and keep their homes every year. Why, because these jesters set the COLA bar lower each and every year. Each and every year it was like taking five or ten percent of a senior's net worth and throwing it away.

After over thirty years of low-balling on cost of living for Social Security Retirement (SSR) increases, it is a fact that many seniors can no longer afford to live on their SSR monthly pension amounts. Democrats have in essence enabled fraudulent cost of living estimates to reduce senior's benefits.

They advocate deceptive methods such as the chained-CPI and the CPI-W, which for the last thirty-years and more have been used to low-ball the SSR COLA calculations. The plan your author and others who care recommend for SSR eliminates this fraud.

You may or may not know that both the *Chained CPI* and *CPI-W* and a few other methods have been the basis for the underhanded SSR COLA for seniors. These have been adjusted downward for years and more seniors are now at the poverty line or below.

A normal human being unfamiliar with government antics designed to hurt seniors would ask, "Why not just use the actual inflation rate instead of the mumbo jumbo from the demented minds of coffee breath college professors?" The questions beg to be answered.

How did it get this way? Think of a bunch of bearded light-minded coffee-breath academicians advising the Democrat Party to stiff seniors on the inflation rate and you will begin to see the picture. . I know this for a fact because for twenty-years I was on the faculty as a peer professor at Marywood University, and Misericordia University, both in Pennsylvania. My experience is that it is even worse than you could imagine.

I'll bet that you will like the recommendations we produce in this book. Your annual SSR increment will come in at a much more realistic number than the 1.6% received in 2020.

How does 11% v 2% sound? The recommendation is better than that. It also makes seniors just about whole again.

In two chapters from now, I hope you all enjoy reading an article that will hit home for all seniors who have noticed, there is little to nothing left after the bills are paid or remain unpaid each month. The Chapter is titled *Social Security Has "Cheated" seniors Out of $15,258 Over the Past Decade.* Enjoy

If you feel like screaming and shouting "finally!" as you read this one, feel free.

Before we get there, however, I am very honored and please to have a contribution from the alternate index calculator himself, Walter J. Williams. I had the pleasure of speaking with this sage economist and much of the facts in this book are based on his copious research. I know you will enjoy reading this chapter almost as much as I enjoy the fact that I can present it to you. *Big Thank you's* to the one & only Walter J. Williams. Thank you, John for this contribution.

It is in the next chapter and it is taken from the publicly available portion of shadowstats.com

Chapter 8 John Williams' Shadow Government Statistics

John Williams'
Shadow Government Statistics
Analysis Behind and Beyond Government Economic Reporting

No. 515—PUBLIC COMMENT
ON INFLATION
MEASUREMENT AND THE
CHAINED-CPI (C-CPI)

April 8, 2013

Click Here for Link to: SPECIAL
SUPPLEMENT—CHAINED-
CPI

Consumer Price Index Has Been Reconfigured Since Early-1980s So As to Understate Inflation versus Common Experience

- CPI no longer measures the cost of maintaining a constant standard of living.

- CPI no longer measures full inflation for out-of-pocket expenditures.

- With the misused cover of academic theory, politicians forced significant underreporting of official inflation, so as to cut annual cost-of-living adjustments to Social Security, etc.

- Politicians look to expand further the concept of artificially-suppressed cost-of-living adjustments in current budget-deficit negotiations, through the use of the Chained-CPI (see Special *C-CPI Supplement* at end of this document).

- Use of the CPI to adjust retirement benefits, private income or to set investment goals impairs the ability of retirees, income earners and investors to stay ahead of inflation.

- Understated inflation used in estimating inflation-adjusted growth has created the illusion of recovery in reported GDP.

PROBLEMS WITH INFLATION ESTIMATION

This public comment updates No. 438—Public Comment on Inflation *of May 15, 2012, reviewing the nature of inflation understatement by the U.S. government's statistical agencies and the rationale and approach used by Shadowstats in compiling the Shadowstats Alternate Consumer Inflation measures. While the following text includes new material, the concepts all have been explored in earlier writings. Most of the prior* Comment *has been repeated, including some material from the September 2008* Response to BLS Article on CPI Misperceptions. *-- John Williams*

Real-World Experience and Public Perceptions versus Academic Theories and Political Gimmicks

In the last 30 years, a growing gap has been obvious between government reporting of inflation, as measured by the consumer price index (CPI), and the perceptions of actual inflation held by the general public. Anecdotal evidence and occasional surveys have indicated that the general public believes inflation is running well above official reporting, and that public perceptions tend to mirror the inflation experience that once was reflected in the government's formal CPI reporting.

The growing difference in perception versus reality primarily is due to changes made over decades as to how the CPI is calculated and defined by the government. Specifically, changes made to the definition of the CPI and related methodology in recent decades have reflected theoretical constructs offered by academia that have little relevance to the real-world use of the CPI by the general public. Importantly, the public usually has not been aware of or understood these changes.

What the Public Looks for in an Inflation Measure

Individual need for and use of a CPI measure generally is tied to personal financial decisions or planning, in terms of wage or income growth/adjustments, contract or benefit price adjustments and/or in terms of targeting financial returns that would stay ahead of inflation.

Accordingly, individuals look to the government's CPI as a measure of the cost of living of maintaining a constant standard of living, as well as measuring that cost of living in terms of out-of-pocket expenses.
Without meeting those parameters, an inflation measure has limited, if any, use for an individual.

Where the CPI at one time met those parameters desired by the public, government efforts turned the CPI away from measuring the price changes in a fixed-weight basket of goods and services, to a quasi- substitution-based basket of goods, which destroyed the concept of the CPI as a measure of the cost of living of maintaining a constant standard of living.

Separately, the use of hedonic quality modeling in adjusting the prices of goods and services destroyed the concept of the CPI as a measure of out-of-pocket expenses. Estimated by computer models, hedonic adjustments alter inflation accounting for nebulous quality changes that cannot otherwise be measured directly and that commonly are not recognized by consumers.

The Way It Was

Measurement of consumer inflation traditionally reflected assessing the cost of maintaining a constant standard of living, as measured by a fixed-basket of goods. Maintaining a constant standard of living, however, is a concept not popular in current economic literature, and certainly not within the thinking or the lexicon of the Bureau of Labor Statistics (BLS), the government's statistical agency that estimates and reports on consumer inflation.

The changing costs of maintaining a constant standard of living were measured by pricing out a fixed-basket of goods and services—same components, same weighting—period after period. Whatever the percentage change was in the cost of that basket of goods, that is how much income would have to rise in order for someone to maintain a fixed- or constant-standard of living over the given period. At least it was a reasonably consistent approximation of same.

Tracking changes in the cost of a fixed-basket of goods was the approach to estimating inflation, going back to at least the 1700s,[i] and prior to 1945, the fixed-basket CPI tracked by the U.S. government actually was known as the Cost of Living Index.[ii]

In the first half of the 20th century, though, the concept of a –constant level of satisfaction‖ evolved in academia, as a –true cost of living‖ concept. The general argument was that changing relative costs of goods would result in consumer substitution of less-expensive goods for more-expensive goods. Allowing for a substitution of goods within the formerly fixed-basket, the maximization of the –utility‖ of money held by consumers would allow attainment of –constant level of satisfaction‖ for the consumer.

This type of inflation-measure is more appropriate for the GDP concept—where it is used today— measuring shifting weightings with actual consumption, rather than with the fixed weightings needed to assess the costs of maintaining a constant standard of living.

Where the substitution-based approach was viewed as impractical for a consumer price index, the fixed-basket approach remained the preferred inflation measure.[iii] The academic thinking in this area remains divided, even today.[iv]

The constant-level-of-satisfaction approach was contrary to the concept of measuring the cost of maintaining a constant-standard-of-living. In the extreme current circumstance, where the average household cannot stay ahead of even official CPI inflation, consider that shifting household preferences from more-expensive to less-expensive products is forced by limited income, or having to shift consumption patterns just to cover necessities. Maintaining a constant-standard-of-living means being able to consume the same goods in the same quantity, without having to trade-off living quality versus price, being able to buy needed gasoline, for example, without having to cut back on food quality.

While the average consumer may not be able to maintain his or her current standard of living, at the moment, it still is of significant value to know what is needed in income growth in order to offset the decline in the standard of living due to actual inflation.

The Way the Politicians Wanted It

In the early-1990s, political Washington moved to change the nature of the CPI. The contention was that the CPI overstated inflation (it did not allow substitution of less-expensive hamburger for more-expensive steak). Both sides of the aisle and the financial media touted the benefits of a ―more-accurate‖ CPI, one that would allow the substitution of goods and services.

The plan was to reduce cost of living adjustments for government payments to Social Security recipients, etc. The cuts in reported inflation were an effort to reduce the federal deficit without anyone in Congress having to do the politically impossible: to vote against Social Security. The inflation-calculation changes had the further benefit to government fiscal conditions of pushing taxpayers artificially into higher tax brackets, thus increasing tax revenues. The changes afoot were publicized, albeit under the cover of academic theories. Few in the public paid any attention.

Katharine G. Abraham, then commissioner of the Bureau of Labor Statistics, laid out her recollections in an August 1996 paper:

―Back in the early winter of 1995, Federal Reserve Board Chairman Alan Greenspan testified before the Congress that he thought the CPI substantially overstated the rate of growth in the cost of living. His testimony generated a considerable amount of discussion. Soon afterwards, Speaker of the House Newt Gingrich, at a town meeting in

Kennesaw, Georgia, was asked about the CPI and responded by saying,

We have a handful of bureaucrats who, all professional economists agree, have an error in their calculations. If they can't get it right in the next 30 days or so, we zero them out, we transfer the responsibility to either the Federal Reserve or the Treasury and tell them to get it right.

A further comment was noted in a 2008 *San Francisco Chronicle* article, ―In the 1990s, for example, Republicans wanted to make changes in calculating inflation along the lines recommended by a special commission, including more use of quality adjustments. By lowering the official inflation rate, such changes promised to reduce the annual cost-of-living adjustments for Social Security and other federal programs.

> [Katherine] Abraham, the Clinton bureau [of Labor Statistics] commissioner, remembers sitting in Republican House Speaker Newt Gingrich's office:

He said to me, *If you could see your way clear to doing these things, we might have more money for BLS programs.*' ‖ [vi]

Federal Reserve Chairman Alan Greenspan and Michael Boskin, then chairman of the Council of Economic Advisors, were very clear as to how changing or ―correcting‖ the CPI calculations would help to reduce the deficit. As described at the time by Robert Hershey of the *New York Times*, ―Speaker Newt Gingrich, Republican of Georgia, suggested this week that fixing the [CPI] index, with its implications for lower spending [Social Security, etc.] and higher revenue [tax bracket adjustments], would provide maneuvering room for budget negotiators …‖ [vii]

> ―Alan Greenspan, chairman of the Federal Reserve, is among the other Government officials who have spoken optimistically about financial benefits of a more accurate [CPI] [viii]

Economists believe one of the most important [CPI upside biases] is when consumers shift their buying patterns in response to changing prices, substituting one product for another. The [CPI] index is based on a fixed market basket of goods and services. But, for example, if the price on an item like steak gets too expensive, consumers may switch to hamburger.‖ ix

The Boskin Commission Report, December 4, 1996, actually used steak and chicken for its substitution example. The examples used in arguing for changing the CPI clearly were tied to prices rising and resulting consumer demand shifting to a lower-quality product. Simply put, that was the destruction of the cost-of-maintaining-a-constant-standard-of-living concept and was the primary consideration of those seeking to change the CPI, although other issues would come into play. The drive here was as to get a lower inflation reading, irrespective of whether the data were —more-accurate.

Summary of Real-World Needs versus Theoretical Constructs of Academia

While the 1990s saw the push to reduce official inflation reporting, by shifting from a fixed-weight to at least a quasi-substitution-based CPI, less-publicized actions were taken to reduce CPI reporting through the introduction of hedonic quality adjustments, starting in the 1980s.

Maintaining Constant Standard of Living (Fixed-Basket Inflation) versus Substitution in CPI

- Since the 1700s, consumer inflation has been estimated by measuring price changes in a fixed- weight basket of goods, effectively measuring the cost of living of maintaining a constant standard of living.

- Allowing substitution of lower-priced and lower-quality goods in the basket (i.e. more hamburger when steak prices rise) lowers the reported rate of inflation versus the fixed-basket measure.

- BLS introduced: Geometric weighting—a purely a mathematical gimmick that automatically reduces the weightings of goods rising in price, and vice versa—it has no demonstrated relationship to consumer substitution of goods based on price changes. It was explained as a surrogate for a substitution measure.

- BLS introduced: More frequent re-weightings of the CPI index from every ten years to every two years, which moved the CPI closer to a substitution-based index, but the change was not considered a change in methodology.

BLS introduced: Ongoing re-weightings of sales outlets (discount/mass-merchandisers versus Main Street shops), also moving closer to a substitution-based index and creating other constant- standard-of-living issues.

Out-of-Pocket Expenses versus Nebulous Quality (Hedonic) Adjustments

- Traditionally, what a consumer paid out-of-pocket for goods and services reflected adjustments for quality changes that could be directly quantified in a monetary sense.
    - Quality adjustments that can be measured directly in price are legitimate, such as measuring the price differential of an eight-ounce candy bar that is reduced in size to six- ounces but remains priced and packaged in the same sized box as the eight-ounce version.

- The BLS expanded quality adjustments to include the concept of ‖hedonic‖ quality adjustments, altering the pricing of goods and services for nebulous quality changes that often were not viewed or recognized by consumers as desired improvements.

- Where the effect here on the pricing of goods and services could not be quantified directly from a pricing standpoint, the pricing impact was estimated by computer statistical modeling—hedonic adjustment modeling—that had little if any relevance to real-world experience.

- Where the quality of the product was deemed by the government to have improved (the usual circumstance), prices in the CPI calculations were adjusted lower to offset the higher quality.

- Usually, though, the purchasing consumer only had the option of paying out-of-pocket the full price for the product, again with little or no concept of the quality improvement being acquired and/or having no chance to opt out of paying for the improvements.

    o In an early example, the government mandated the use of a gasoline formulation that purportedly would improve auto emissions. That added ten cents per gallon to gasoline costs, but that cost was excluded from CPI calculations. The person filling his or her gas tank, however, suffered the actual out-of-pocket expense.

    o The government later abandoned excluding government-mandated ‖quality‖ improvements, such as gasoline additives, from inflation calculations, but the principles here were exactly the same for industry-generated ‖quality‖ improvements that were not optional to consumers.

    o Text books, for example were modeled, where one pricing factor in the hedonic quality model was whether or not there were color pictures in a book. Unless the student was an art student, the concern usually was not over colored pictures, but rather along the lines of
    ‖What is my out-of-pocket cost for textbooks this semester?‖

    o New computer features usually were deemed quality improvements, with downside price adjustments made in the CPI for the changes, even though a consumer may not have wanted or used the features.

The consumer still had to buy those features and pay full cost out-of-pocket, irrespective of what the government determined those products were generating in purported hedonic quality benefits that the consumer was not considering or using.

- o Significant feature changes should be treated as a new product introduction, or otherwise ignored.

- If the use of the hedonic process were legitimate here, it would be applied to all goods and services, but a CPI, so based, soon would become meaningless to the public (as already has happened with the CPI-U).

  - o For example, there has been no pricing adjustment (upside in this case) to the costs of air travel for the destruction of travel convenience with the advent of the TSA, or from the downward spiral in U.S. air traveler comfort and convenience resulting from the effects of mergers and acquisitions, and from increasing flight delays due to economizing on aircraft maintenance.

- Consumer concerns are for his or her out-of-pocket expenses. What am I paying for my textbooks this semester; what am I paying out-of-pocket to fly from New York to Chicago; or what am I paying out-of-pocket for a computer, even if I am looking just to use limited functions but have no choice but to buy unwanted features?

What The Changes Did to Inflation

The following chart shows the detail of two CPI series and the impact that various methodological changes have made on reported series. Beyond the ―Year‖ column, the first column is the annual average index level for the CPI-U-RS series, which is an experimental series published by the Bureau of Labor Statistics that goes back in time, estimating the annual inflation rate as if all the methodological changes made to the CPI during the last 35 years had been in place since day one. The second column (1) is the annual inflation indicated by the CPI-U-RS series. The third column is the headline CPI-U series as published the BLS, the fourth column (2) is the annual inflation indicated by the CPI-U series.

The fifth column [(1)-(2)], is the difference that the methodological changes made in the given year, versus the annual headline CPI-U number, and the sixth column is the cumulative annual shortfall in the CPI-U created by the various methodological changes. The cumulative number flattens out after 1999, because all the significant methodological changes counted in the CPU-I-RS were in place by then.

Nonetheless, there were additional changes, although they were not deemed to be methodological by the BLS, as discussed in the next section.

Shadow Government Statistics — No. 515—Public Comment on Inflation / Chained-CPI, April 8, 2013

Net Reduction in CPI-U Inflation from Changes in Methodology
As Reflected in the CPI-U-RS versus CPI-U Series (1980 to 2011)
Table Described in Text following, Sources: ShadowStats, BLS

	(1)			(2)		(1)-(2)	Cumulative
	Average CPI-U-RS	CPI-U-RS		Average CPI-U	CPI-U	Change in Annual	Annual Inflation
Year	Dec 97=100	Yr/Yr		'82-4=100	Yr/Yr	Inflation*	Shortfall
1980	127.1			82.4			0
1981	139.2	9.5%		90.9	10.3%	-0.8%	-0.8%
1982	147.6	6.0%		96.5	6.2%	-0.1%	-0.9%
1983	153.9	4.3%		99.6	3.2%	1.1%	0.1%
1984	160.2	4.1%		103.9	4.3%	-0.2%	-0.1%
1985	165.7	3.4%		107.6	3.6%	-0.1%	-0.2%
1986	168.7	1.8%		109.6	1.9%	0.0%	-0.3%
1987	174.4	3.4%		113.6	3.6%	-0.3%	-0.5%
1988	180.8	3.7%		118.3	4.1%	-0.5%	-1.0%
1989	188.6	4.3%		124.0	4.8%	-0.5%	-1.5%
1990	198.0	5.0%		130.7	5.4%	-0.4%	-1.9%
1991	205.1	3.6%		136.2	4.2%	-0.6%	-2.5%
1992	210.3	2.5%		140.3	3.0%	-0.5%	-3.0%
1993	215.5	2.5%		144.5	3.0%	-0.5%	-3.5%
1994	220.1	2.1%		148.2	2.6%	-0.4%	-4.0%
1995	225.4	2.4%		152.4	2.8%	-0.4%	-4.4%
1996	231.4	2.7%		156.9	3.0%	-0.3%	-4.7%
1997	236.4	2.2%		160.5	2.3%	-0.1%	-4.8%
1998	239.7	1.4%		163.0	1.6%	-0.2%	-5.0%
1999	244.7	2.1%		166.6	2.2%	-0.1%	-5.1%
2000	252.9	3.4%		172.2	3.4%	0.0%	-5.1%
2001	260.0	2.8%		177.1	2.8%	0.0%	-5.2%
2002	264.2	1.6%		179.9	1.6%	0.0%	-5.1%
2003	270.1	2.2%		184.0	2.3%	0.0%	-5.2%
2004	277.4	2.7%		188.9	2.7%	0.0%	-5.1%
2005	286.7	3.4%		195.3	3.4%	0.0%	-5.2%
2006	296.1	3.3%		201.6	3.2%	0.1%	-5.1%
2007	304.5	2.8%		207.3	2.8%	0.0%	-5.1%
2008	316.2	3.8%		215.3	3.8%	0.0%	-5.1%
2009	315.0	-0.4%		214.5	-0.4%	0.0%	-5.1%
2010	320.2	1.7%		218.1	1.6%	0.0%	-5.1%
2011	330.3	3.2%		224.9	3.2%	0.0%	-5.1%
Aggregate Methodological CPI-U Reduction						-5.1%	

* Totals vary due to rounding

Copyright 2013 American Business Analytics & Research, LLC, www.shadowstats.com

The substitution-related alterations to inflation methodologies were made beginning in the mid-1990s. The introduction of major hedonic concepts began in the 1980s. The aggregate impact of the reporting changes since 1980 has been to reduce the reported level of annual CPI inflation by roughly seven percentage points, where 5.1 percentage points come from the BLS's published estimates of the effects of the individual methodological changes on inflation, shown in the preceding table. The balance comes from ShadowStats estimates of the changes not formally estimated by the BLS. The effects are cumulative going forward in time.

With the support of academic expertise affirming the correctness of the new methodologies, the effects of the reduction in the pace of reported inflation and in the related spiking of reported inflation-adjusted economic growth, have been discussed openly at different times. Consider examples from the 1999 Economic Report of the President Report (Report). x
—A final reason for the slowing of reported price indexes has been methodological changes to both the CPI and the indexes used in the national income accounts. In general, these changes have reduced the measured rate of inflation. For the CPI, methodological changes made from 1995 through 1998 reduced the rate of inflation by about 0.44 percentage point. Changes to be introduced in 1999 and 2000 will reduce it by an additional 0.24 percentage point.‖ Again, these are cumulative changes going forward.

The Report continued, describing the benefits of reduced inflation rate reporting in adding to reported GDP growth, —The BEA [Bureau of Economic Analysis] has also recently switched [1997] from using the CPI to using the producer price index (PPI) to deflate physicians' services and the services of government and for-profit hospitals.

Because the PPI measures of these prices have been increasing less than the comparable CPIs, the changes reduce the rate of increase of the chain-weighted price index for GDP and raise real [inflation-adjusted] GDP growth. These changes, in addition to those passed through from the CPI, will have cumulated to raise the annual growth rate of real GDP by 0.29 percentage point by 2000.‖

That cumulative pace of new boosts to the GDP growth for those several years really should have been 0.54 percentage point, accounting for new hedonic adjustments.xi

Keep in mind that the CPI changes of 0.68% were an aggregate for those years and had to be carried forward—added back in—on a cumulative basis if one wanted to remove the effects of the methodological changes from future data. Against the aggregated 0.68% reduction in the reported inflation, the BLS's related CPI-U-RS series showed an aggregated reduction in the reported inflation of 0.7%, as discussed in the next two sections.

Measuring the Methodological Impacts Going Backward and Forward in Time

The BLS has created what they call the CPI-U-RS (RS stands for research series), designed to restate inflation history as if all the current substitution and hedonic adjustment methodological changes always had been in place. Limited effects of the artificially lowered historical inflation rate can be seen with the following graph.

The narrow red line shows median household income, deflated by the CPI-U-RS, as having been much stronger than the series shown by the thicker blue line, which was deflated by the higher inflation in the traditional CPI-U. The CPI-U versus the CPI-U-RS is detailed in the table.

Shadow Government Statistics — No. 515—Public Comment on Inflation / Chained-CPI, Apri

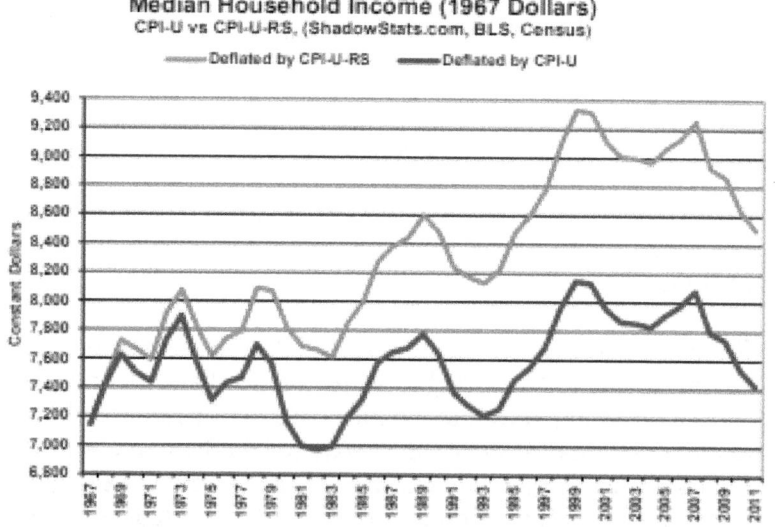

While the differences in recent patterns (post-1999), may appear to be fixed, that is because the CPI-U since 1999 already included the bulk of the changes in the RS series, so the CPI-U-RS and CPI-U

largely are identical in terms of year-to-year change in the post-1999 period. In the earlier years, the changes average less than half of a percent, but those changes reflect the incremental decline in annual inflation triggered by the various methodological changes.

Reverse-engineering the CPI-U-RS so as to reconstruct the CPI-U, as if the various changes had not been made, requires carrying forward the effects of the changes on a cumulative basis. The cumulative effect is seen in the last column of the earlier table.

ShadowStats-Alternate Consumer Inflation Measures

The ShadowStats-Alternate Consumer Inflation Measures were created by reverse-engineering the CPI-U- RS series, and adding in estimates of the inflation effects of factors not otherwise estimated by the BLS, such as more-frequent (two-years versus ten-years) reweighting of the CPI series.

The two ShadowStats series are based on the methodologies in place as of 1980, and separately as of 1990. The estimated lost inflation is added back in, over time, as described in the methodology (1980- based) published each month in the *Commentary* that covers the CPI reporting:

The ShadowStats-Alternate Consumer Inflation Measure adjusts on an additive basis for the cumulative impact on the annual inflation rate of various methodological changes made by the BLS (the series is note calculated). Over the decades, the BLS has altered the meaning of the CPI from being a measure of the cost of living needed to maintain a constant standard of living, to something that neither reflects the constant-standard-of-living concept nor measures adequately most of what consumers view as out-of-pocket expenditures.

Roughly five percentage points of the additive ShadowStats adjustment reflect the BLS's formal estimates of the annual impact of methodological changes; roughly two percentage points reflect changes by the BLS, where ShadowStats has estimated the impact from changes not otherwise published by the BLS.

The Differences Are Large

The approach here is simple, and some argue that the inflation differential since 1980—suggested by the BLS's own estimates—is too large to be realistic. The numbers are what they are, and refinement to the approach certainly is possible. Keep in mind, though, that the differences here are in weighting and in quality adjustments, not in the underlying surveying of raw prices. While some might argue the magnitude of the inflation-understatement, resulting from the historical changes, there is no question as to the understatement of inflation.

If the methodological changes did not reduce CPI inflation reporting meaningfully, the politicians would not have pushed the changes of recent decades, and they would not be pushing now for a ‒new‖ fully- substitution-based and weaker C-CPI in current budget negotiations. In contrast to the highly touted fully-substitution-based C-CPI, the existing CPI is only quasi-substitution based (see the *Special Supplement—C-CPI*). The earlier changes had the impact desired by the politicians. Without them, Social Security checks would be more than double what they are today.

Homeowners' Equivalent Rent, or Hedonic Adjustments to Imaginary Numbers. On the weighting front, it is worth considering that fully 24.0% of the total current CPI-U inflation reporting reflects the category of ‒homeowners' equivalent rent of residences.‖ Instead of reflecting some measure of home prices, as was the case before 1983, the BLS estimates the cost of housing based on what homeowners theoretically would pay to themselves in order to rent their own homes from themselves. The BLS then estimates how much homeowners raise the rent on themselves each month. Starting in 1989, the BLS ‒improved‖ these estimates by beginning to adjust that imaginary series for hedonic quality adjustments.

ShadowStats Alternate CPI Measures. The following graphs show the respective alternate CPI-U series as estimated on both 1980-based and 1990-based methodologies. The latest versions of these graphs always are available on the *Alternate Data* tab on www.shadowstats.com.

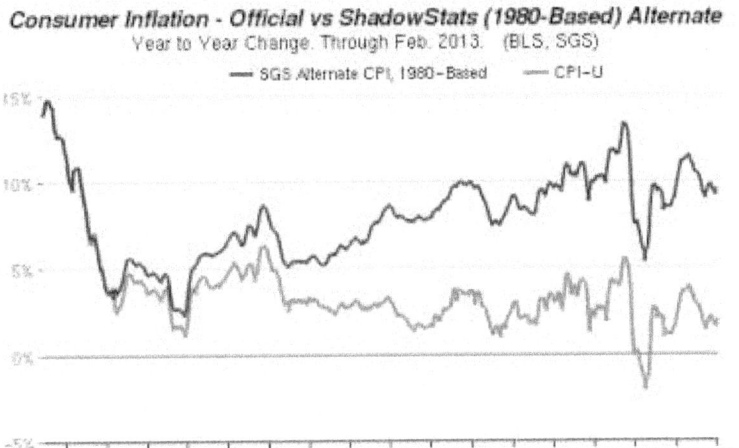

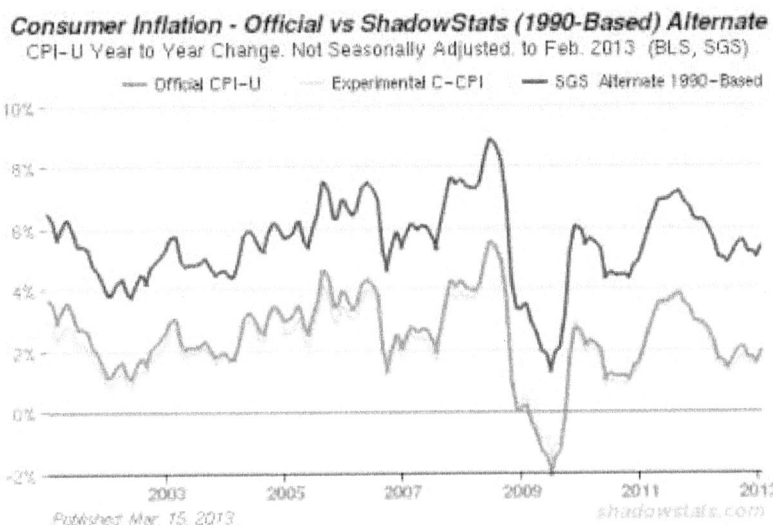

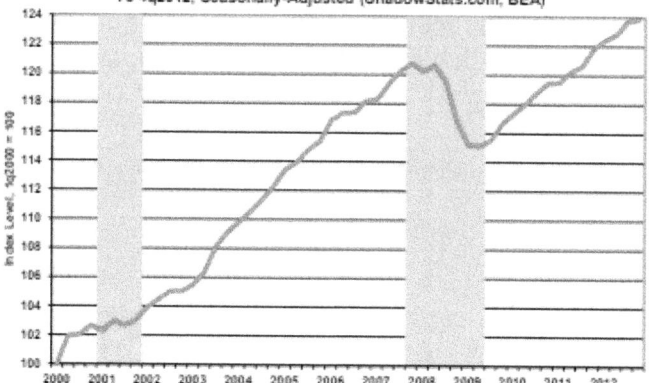

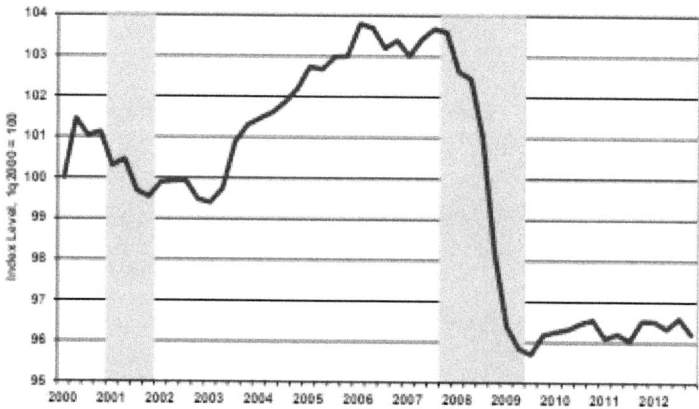

Artificially-Low Inflation Estimates Have Created the Illusion of Recovery

Separately, to varying degrees, artificially-depressed inflation rates have created misleading indications of economic growth in major economic series, including the GDP, industrial production and real retail sales, as deflated by the appropriate inflation measures. This is discussed in some detail in *Hyperinflation 2012*, with assumptions discussed in Chapter 5, beginning on page 38.

Corrected Gross Domestic Product. Consider, for example, gross domestic product (GDP)—the government's broadest estimate of economic activity. Deflated by the GDP's implicit price deflator, not the CPI-U, the full economic recovery indicated by the GDP remains an illusion. It is a statistical illusion created by using too-low a rate of inflation in deflating (removing inflation effects) from the GDP series. The following two graphs tell that story, through the final reporting of fourth-quarter 2012 GDP.

In the first graph, official real (inflation-adjusted) GDP activity has been reported above pre-2007 recession levels—in full recovery—since fourth-quarter 2011 and has shown sustained growth since. No other major economic series has shown a parallel pattern of full economic recovery and beyond. Either the GDP reporting is wrong, or all other major economic series are wrong.

While the GDP is heavily modeled, imputed, theorized and gimmicked, it also encompasses reporting from those various major economic series and private surveys, which attempt to mirror real-world activity. In a related area, the 2001 recession has disappeared from GDP reporting, contrary to other major economic series. Flaws in the GDP inflation methodologies have created the ‒recovery‖ and erased the previous recession.

The second graph plots the GDP corrected for the inflation understatement inherent the GDP deflator of roughly two-percentage points of annual inflation. That inflation understatement resulted from hedonic- quality adjustments, again, as discussed in Hyperinflation 2012.

Note that the 2001 recession is back, and that the —2007‖ recession really started in 2006, consistent with the downturn in the housing market. The economy plunged through 2008 into 2009. Instead of rebounding to full recovery, as seen in the headline GDP, however, the corrected real GDP has been bottom-bouncing, stagnant at a low level of activity. It now is turning down again. The corrected version appears to be much closer to the reality of common experience.

SPECIAL SUPPLEMENT— CHAINED-CPI

PLEASE NOTE: The following material and comments have been extracted and re-edited from recent regular Commentaries *on www.ShadowStats.com.*

An Opinion on the Renewed Push to Use the C-CPI for COLA, Inflation Indexing

The Chained-CPI (C-CPI) is a fully-substitution-based version of the CPI-U, which is the primary inflation measure published by the U.S. government's Bureau of Labor Statistics. The C-CPI is designed to reduce the level of reported inflation that otherwise would be used by individuals to make decisions tied to their investments and income. As a vehicle for artificially reducing COLA adjustments for such programs as Social Security, its proposed use here appears to be a rare area of agreement between both sides in the current budget-deficit negotiations.

Those in the federal government who are honest and forthright with the American public—at least about the proposal to understate the official rate of inflation for purposes of budget reduction—have failed to drive a wooden stake through the heart of the C-CPI. Arising from its second, premature political burial, the C-CPI looks again like it has a strong chance of being used as a new federal parasite to drain consumer liquidity. Like a vampire bat that sucks only enough blood for self-nourishment—leaving its victims alive for further abuse—the use of the C-CPI as a cost-of-living adjustment (COLA) measure is designed to suck real disposable income from the limited cash-flow of Social Security recipients, for the benefit of politicians who do not have the guts to vote against Social Security.

Those receiving, or who will be receiving Social Security payments were forced to pay into the system for all of their working lives, and generally believed the U.S. government would treat them fairly and honestly. The bloodsuckers in Washington have hit their victims similarly, before, back in the 1980s with the introduction of hedonic-quality adjustments to inflation, and in the 1990s with the change of concept in the CPI to a quasi-substitution-based inflation measure. Previously, the CPI measured inflation for a fixed-weight basket of goods, which measured COLAs as an inflation adjustment needed to maintain a constant standard of living.

As noted earlier in this missive, these methodological changes have altered the CPI-U and its more narrowly defined variant, the CPI-W, so that they no longer measure those costs of maintaining a constant standard of living (substitution effects) and no longer measure out-of-pocket costs (hedonic-adjustment effects). Without the changes made to CPI calculations of the last several decades, Social Security payments would be more than double what they are today. Indeed, with the use of a substitution-based index (the C-CPI is fully substitution based), the resulting cost of living adjustments promise only a declining standard of living. Expanding the example that former Federal Reserve Chairman Alan Greenspan often used, where, as the price of steak rose, consumers would shift to hamburger, so too with higher hamburger costs have some cash-strapped retirees actually shifted consumption to dog food.

The President and Congress must address Social Security and other programs, such as Medicare, restructuring them so as make them solvent over the long haul, eliminating the horrendous levels of unfunded liabilities that are deteriorating at an aggregate pace in excess of $5 trillion per year on a net- present-value basis (see the *Hyperinflation Report*). With discussions instead focusing on using the outright deceit of implementing the C-CPI to cut COLA, those controlling the government appear to lack the political will to make needed changes in a straight-forward manner. Under those circumstances, there can be no meaningful budget deal structured by the negotiators in Washington.

The government must be honest with its citizens. If the government cannot afford to pay full COLAs, it is better to indicate that upfront, rather than to try to fool individuals as to the actual level of inflation they have to overcome in order to maintain their living standards. Cutting benefits by stealth and deceit may be politically expedient for the miscreants playing this game, but it is utterly unconscionable.

Beyond the damage caused by the C-CPI not reflecting out-of-pocket costs, and no longer measuring the cost of living of maintaining a constant standard of living, the C-CPI is not a practical measure for being used as a COLA or other benchmark inflation measure.

No Fixed Index Level for Reliable Cost Escalations in Contracts.
As a separate issue, beyond the C-CPI not reflecting the cost of living of maintaining a constant standard of living or of reflecting full out-of- pocket consumer expenses, it cannot be published on a timely-enough basis to make it feasible as an annual-COLA factor.

The following graph shows the regular net revisions to year-to-year inflation in the Chained-CPI, published February 21, 2013 for the years 2011 and 2012. In contrast, the CPI-U and CPI-W never are revised on a not-seasonally-adjusted basis (barring an outright error in calculation).

That feature enables the use of the CPI-U and CPI-W as inflation-adjustment and cost-of-living- adjustment (COLA) measures in contracts, COLA adjustments to Social Security, etc. Although designed as a consumer-damaging, budget-cutting replacement for the CPI-W in government COLA adjustments, the C-CPI reporting is unstable, since it goes through regular revisions every year, for the two prior years. As shown in the following graph, the latest revisions would have suggested an upside revision of about three-tenths of a percentage point to any COLA adjustment would have been made previously for 2011.

As discussed by the BLS in its February 21, 2013 press release:
–Because the current expenditure data required for the calculation of the C-CPI-U are available only with a time lag, the index is issued first in preliminary form, using the latest available expenditure data at the time of publication, and is subject to two subsequent revisions. Therefore, C-CPI-U indexes for the 12 months of 2011 [now] are issued in final form – employing monthly expenditure weights from 2011. Values for the 12 months of 2012 are revised and issued as interim, using expenditure weights from the 2009-2010 period. Calculation of the initial value of the January 2013 C-CPI-U index, and all subsequent months in 2013, will also be based upon 2009-2010 ex

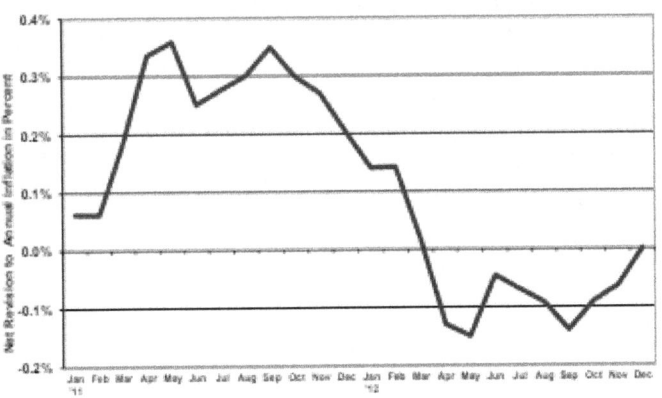

Notes on Different Measures of the Consumer Price Index

The Consumer Price Index (CPI) is the broadest inflation measure published by the U.S. Government, through the Bureau of Labor Statistics (BLS), Department of Labor:

*The **CPI-U (Consumer Price Index for All Urban Consumers)** is the monthly headline inflation number (seasonally adjusted) and is the* broadest in its coverage, representing the buying patterns of all urban consumers. Its standard measure is not seasonally adjusted, and it never is revised on that basis except for outright errors.

The **CPI-W (CPI for Urban Wage Earners and Clerical Workers)** covers the more-narrow universe of urban wage earners and clerical workers and is used in determining cost of living adjustments in government programs such as Social Security. Otherwise, its background is the same as the CPI-U.

The **C-CPI-U (Chain-Weighted CPI-U)** is an experimental measure, where the weighting of components is fully substitution based. It generally shows lower annual inflation rate than the CPI-U and CPI-W. The latter two measures once had fixed weightings—so as to measure the cost of living of maintaining a constant standard of living—but now are quasi-substitution-based. Since it is fully substitution based, the series tends to reflect lower inflation than the other CPI measures. Accordingly, the C-CPI-U is the "new inflation" measure being considered by Congress and the White House as a tool for reducing Social Security cost-of-living adjustments by stealth.

The **ShadowStats Alternative CPI-U Measures** are attempts at adjusting reported CPI-U inflation for the impact of methodological change of recent decades designed to move the concept of the CPI away from being a measure of the cost of living needed to maintain a constant standard of living. There are two measures, where the first is based on reporting methodologies in place as of 1980, and the second is based on reporting methodologies in place as of 1990.

Notes:

[i] Fixler, Dennis, Bureau of Labor Statistics, ―The Consumer Price Index: underlying concepts and caveats,‖ *Monthly Labor Review*, December 1993.

[ii] Schmidt, Mary Lynn, Bureau of Labor Statistics, ―Comparing market basket changes and the CPI,‖ 1995.

[iii] Ulmer, Melville T., ―On the Theory of Cost of Living Index Numbers,‖ *Journal of the American Statistical Association*, Vol. 41, No. 236 (December 1946), pp. 530-542.

[iv] National Research Council, *At What Price? Conceptualizing and Measuring Cost-of-Living and Price Indexes*, (2002).

[v] Abraham, Katharine G., Bureau of Labor Statistics, ―Statistics Under the Spotlight: Improving the Consumer Price Index: Statement,‖ Paper presented at a meeting of the American Statistical Association, Chicago, Illinois, August 6, 1996.

[vi] Zuckerman, Sam, ‒Government's economic data misleading, he says,‖ *San Francisco Chronicle*, May 25, 2008.

[vii] Hershey, Robert D., Jr., ‒Panel Sees a Corrected Price Index as Deficit-Cutter,‖ *New York Times,* September 15, 1995.

[viii] *Ibid.*

[ix] *Ibid.*

[x] ‒Inflation: Flat or Falling,‖ *Economic Report of the President 1999*, pp. 87-95.

[xi] ‒Comparing growth in GDP and labour productivity: measurement issues,‖ OECD, December 2007.

Chapter 9 Social Security "Cheated" Seniors $15,258 in Past Decade

SSR purchasing power falling at alarming rate

This chapter is based on an article by Sean Williams writing for Motley Fool just about three years ago in October 2019. He first announced like me, that seniors got another rip-off-calculated COLA from the Democrats in government along with the coffee-breath beauties in academe. It was the annual announcement which occurs in the middle of October--Social Security's most anticipated announcement of the year was put out again and now is almost two years in the past.

The message is that things will not be getting much better for seniors. Need it or not, all recipients were going to get a mouth-watering *"generous"* 1.6% bump. Isn't life just grand? If this is your eleventh raise, Using the real inflation rate, Sean Williams has news for you that will put a big tear in your eye. The analysts in the Bureau of Labor Statistics (BLS) from academe and government, using their CPI-W recipe for fraud, over the last ten years have stolen an average $15,258 from you and every other SSR recipient in the past decade. Think about whether you and other seniors should ever trust the government again,

It all happened on Oct. 10, 2019 when the U.S. Bureau of Labor Statistics (BLS) released inflation data from September, which happened to be the final puzzle piece needed for the "experts" to calculate the various CPI rates which ultimately determine the Social Security Retirement's (SSR) cost-of-living adjustment (COLA) for 2020.

In simple terms, COLA is the "raise" that SSR beneficiaries receive from one year to the next that takes into account the inflation they've faced. Of course, it's not a raise in the truest sense of the word, because COLA is only designed to keep up with inflation, not outpace it.

When the news release crossed the wire, we learned seniors from across America had begun figuratively to get sick to their stomachs. And, of course there was a run on Pepto-Bismol at Seven-Elevens.

OK I jest. But this is not far from the mark. I know it sickened me as I do get sick when I am ripped off by anybody, especially the government. It is almost 100% certain that the program's nearly 64 million beneficiaries will receive their hard-fought 1.6% raise per month on the average per month for 2020. What is not certain is whether they can find a store that still takes pennies so that they will be able to spend their wad each month.

For those calculating your increase, save your grey matter as Sean Williams did the calculation for us all. He predicts that the number is about $24.00 per month extra for the average retired worker. Isn't Uncle Sam the greatest?

Sean is a fair minded guy so he admits in his piece written for motleyfool.com that this $24.00 bonanza does not tell the full story of Social Security's COLA. Over the past decade, this yearly paltry increase has cost seniors a lot of money. About that I am not kidding. That's a sanitized way of saying that the government, based on the committee of Democrat analysts in government and coffee-breath professors in academe, stole $15,258 out of the pockets of each and every senior citizen in the last decade. Did you complain about your loss? It is OK if you did not. I know most did not see the loss but surely we all felt it.

Williams does not let on but since his article was published, senior citizens receiving as little as zero percent per year during the Obama Administration, as a group had never complained to the cheating perpetrators in the government who committed this major crime.

I do think that if seniors would let the "bums" in Congress know they are really ruffled," and that they are no longer going to vote for their regular Congress-persons, I predict that something good would begin to happen for seniors. Congress-persons who stiff seniors are not worthy of being reelected.

Reelecting such louts is not the answer for seniors to be able to make ends meet and make mortgage payments. The Congress is on the other side folks. Unless you are willing to kick them out of office, things will definitely stay the same.

Why? Sean Williams says "The CPI-W is inherently flawed"

Social Security's COLA has been determined by the Consumer Price Index for Urban Wage Earners and Clerical Workers, or CPI-W, since 1975. To put this in perspective, it is a swindle calculation. It is designed so the government can exploit seniors who collect SSR, thereby save the rest of the taxpayers money. That money comes right out of senior's pockets and it mounts quickly.

The CPI-W index is devised so seniors cannot understand it and will not try. It is an index with eight major spending categories and countless subcategories. It is complex so you cannot understand it without a lawyer. The lawyer won't save you any money but they can explain why you are losing so much each year. Short of firing the Congress)great idea), or pleading your 2021 case to President Biden, there is not much you can do about it. Firing the louts in office would make you feel better.

Each of the subcategories has a predetermined weighting that allows the BLS to express aggregate inflation in one simple and concise number each month. When it comes to Social Security's COLA, only the readings from the third quarter (July through September) factor into the calculation.

The coffee breath professors and key Democrat government official analysts were never before, and still are not, interested in providing a fair representation of the inflation rate, or they would simply use the actual inflation rate. Dah! This rate is available across the Internet in many places. Two of my favorites are Shadowstats.com and Chapwoodindex.com. It is amazing how the government has intentionally ripped off the elderly community. Watch that you do not get too angry.

The machination which the experts decided is their baby is called the CPI-W. The W stands for *worker* even though SSR recipients are retired and do not work. You figure that one out. Experts on inflation who do not have a dog in the hunt concluded years ago that the CPI-W does an awful job at representing the true inflation that seniors face every day. Consequently each and every year seniors are shortchanged when they received their skinned down COLA Their loss is not theoretical. It can be counted in real dollars.

Congress has been aware for years that seniors are getting squeezed unfairly but the Congress has chosen not to fix the problem. Why? Because seniors rarely complain and it helps to balance the budget. You can bet that it is more of the former than the latter as seniors have not been complaining enough to make it worth Congress's while to effect a real change.

Here is one of the excuses they give. They say it is because, as the name of the index implies (*the dash W part*) , it's measuring the spending habits of urban and clerical *workers*, many of whom are not 62 or older, nor are they receiving a Social Security retirement benefit.

In short, urban and clerical workers spend their money very differently than senior citizens spend their smaller amounts. Despite knowing this, Congress keeps the fraudulent extortion going. Congress simply has no time for seniors who choose not to complain.

Although apples-to-apples comparisons are hard to come by, the BLS did compare expenditures using the CPI-W and an experimental index known as the Consumer Price Index for the Elderly (CPI-E) in December 2011. Your author suggests that if given the opportunity to speak up, all seniors reject and of the BLS CPI dash measurements, including the W, the U, the E, and the chained version of the CPI. Do not buy into their charade. Reject all of the BLS work.

The CPI-E measure is not in effect. It is still experimental. However, it will if ever it is implemented, produce an inexact measurement of the real inflation rate. Its only claim to fame so far is that if it were substituted for the CPI-W, it would measure the spending habits of households with persons 62 and older.

Despite this alternate measurement being better than CPI-W, even with this Congress continues to cheat seniors—just not as much as the other CPI's such as CPI-W and the Chained CPI. Congress can create legislation to make life better for those in most need of a fair shake by taking away all the hocus pocus and merely creating an inflation rate based on real market conditions as we had until the corrupt BLS got in the act.

In their test case, what the BLS found was that CPI-E spending on medical care was double that of the CPI-W, with housing costs also notably higher. This tells us that the CPI-W has always been regularly underweighting the true inflation that seniors actually contend with in regard to medical care and housing costs.

It does grant higher weighting to categories that don't matter much to seniors, such as apparel and the cost of a college or university education. Nonetheless, it, too is a contrivance to keep the BLS lording over seniors. Advise Congress to reject it and go back to the market basket year-to-year comparison.

The lack of believability in any government index is a very big problem considering that more than 4 out of 5 Social Security recipients are at least 62 years old. Not one member of Congress has stepped up and said that they know how to solve the problem and that they will solve the problem for seniors. I know how to solve it and I have solved it in numerous chapters in this book and other books that I have written about the subject. Would somebody please tell the current president that the solution to his troubles on the COLA for seniors is right here in this book.

Seniors lost major purchasing power because of Congress in last ten years.

The Senior Citizens League has been working on this for a long time. With 1.2 million supporters, The Senior Citizens League (TSCL) is one of the nation's largest nonpartisan seniors' groups.

Their mission is to promote and assist members and supporters, to educate and alert senior citizens about their rights and freedoms as U.S. Citizens, and to protect and defend the benefits senior citizens have earned and paid for. TSCL is not a friend of our do-nothing Congress. Instead, it consists of vocally active senior citizens concerned about the protection of their Social Security, Medicare, and veteran or military retiree benefits.

The group was first established as a special project—The Enlisted Association on January 1, 1995. At this time, TSCL became an independent 501[c][4] citizens' action organization.

Sean Williams noted that according to a news analysis from The Senior Citizens League (TSCL), extremely low COLAs over the past decade have cost retired workers a fortune. Whereas COLAs averaged 3% over the previous decade, the past 10 years have seen the average annual COLA dip to 1.4%. This includes three instances in Obama Times where no COLA was passed along in 2010, 2011, and 2016 due to what the Democrats called "deflation." My response to that is the name of one of my favorite animals—Bull.

Obama's administration created records in its propensity to stiff seniors out of a proper inflation-based COLA. For example, it was also responsible for the lowest positive COLA in COLA history—a meager 0.3% increase from Obama's team in 2017. And then, last year, approximately half of all beneficiaries saw no real increase as Social Security's 2.8% COLA was gobbled up by increases to Medicare Part B premiums. There have been no big surprises for seniors as their possible spending trajectory points to the floor.

To show you in some real numbers why the CPI-W is a rip-off, remember last year's "big" 2.8% COLA disappeared because of Medicare Part B since medical is not included in CPI-W. This year, the supplemental insurance as well as Medicare Part D put a lot of seniors into the poor-house. I was close and if this book is successful, maybe I can avoid the poor house again next year.

Pardon the boredom but this is true and exact

Here are the specifics. My Humana Pharmacy policy last year was about $28.00 per month per person. This year the same policy is $56.00. It doubled perfectly. This doubling ate up the total of the $24.00 COLA and added another $4.00 per month in out of pocket expenses. To be frank, at this point, the COLA was

G-O-N-E!

Since my wife also has Humana, she has to come up with her own $4.00 per month also. For both of us together, the cost is $8.00 X 12 months == $96.00 out of pocket for the family for the year. Not only was the COLA not enough for Pharmacy (Medicare Part D) but there is not a dime left for any other inflationary increases such as food price increases and clothing increases, taxes, and other insurances. The government inflation system is a lousy system i .

Of course that is not all. Last year our AARP supplemental from United Health Care was $187 00 or $374 for both my wife and me. This year, it is $202.00 per month each or $404.00 for both of us. So, this year, we owe another $40.00 per month more (40 X12 = $480 for the year.) Since the $24.00 COLA was already eaten up by the Humana Pharmacy, there was no COLA left to apply to this extra $40.00 per month due to United Health Care Supplemental Medicare increase. Pat and I had to absorb it ourselves from zero increases from any source. Eventually, after a few years of this, people run out of money. Why? One word:

G-O-V-E-R-N-M-E-N-T

Out of nowhere, with no COLAs left, and no other pension increases, and no job at 73 years of age, my wife and I have to absorb $480.00 for a Medicare Supplemental policy. Seniors in our situation are asking themselves. *How are we supposed to pay for this?* My wife and I have similar sentiments. *How are we supposed to pay for this?* I sure hope this book is successful to help our own bottom-line expenses.

Remember COLA is supposed to be the "raise" that we as SSR beneficiaries receive from one year to the next. It is supposed to take into account every dime of the inflation that seniors have faced. Seniors are not supposed to have lots of extra out of pocket expenses because we are not to receive anything extra. Why?

Because the COLA is not a raise in the truest sense of the word. COLA is only designed to keep up with inflation, not outpace it. As noted in our case, and in all previous years, with the bogus CPI calculations from the BLS it does not even keep up with inflation. Recently, the facts show that it gives less and less and less when seniors are looking from a last-year's perspective for same, same, and same. There is never a chance for more, more and more.

If the government were not using the CPI-W, the Medicare premiums would have been factored into the formula as well as the Pharma costs and the Medicare Supplemental. For my wife and I to break even, we would need a very good CPI-E COLA or my recommendation to the president and Congress—Dear President Trump, please fix this.

Unfortunately, in creating the CPI-W, the coffee-breath professors from academe, the Congress and the Democrat government BLS analysts were not interested in helping seniors so it is what it is.

More specifically, Social Security policy analyst Mary Johnson at TSCL found that the purchasing power of Social Security dollars has declined substantially over the past 10 years. [No kidding Mary!]

In dollar terms, Johnson notes that a retiree with a small average benefit of $1,075 a month in 2009 has lost $15,258 in financial growth between 2010 and 2019 because of the aforementioned 1.4% average COLA, when compared with what a 3% average COLA would have delivered.

Blame Congress and the Democrat government analysts whose mission is to reduce the federal deficit by stiffing seniors. Don't forget to save a second dose of blame for the coffee-breath professors who teach our children to stiff the elderly at every opportunity, especially if they support Donald Trump in his role as President of the United States of America.

If Congress and the regulatory bodies who are supposed to honestly determine the actual inflation rate, choose not to do their jobs correctly, what should the people do. While seniors are being stiffed overtly by these people, their loss of purchasing power is even more striking when we look back further over the years.

This is not a new phenomenon. seniors have always been threatened by Democrats, one election after another. Now there are no threats; instead the Democrats simply retaliate against seniors for their nerve to love their God and for God's love of President Donald J. Trump.

If you are not yet sick of my proof that government and academe delivered this "screw job" to the elderly, I have more proof. Over the past decade, what $100 in Social Security income once bought for retired workers will now only purchase $67 worth of those same goods and services. Congress knows this. Ask your Congress person if they care an iota. FYI, let's define iota so we all know: *an extremely small amount.*

TSCL's analysis says that a COLA should never average lower than 3% in any year to lessen the drain of retirement savings on seniors, and in order to keep the elderly out of poverty.

Chapter 9 Social Security "Cheated Seniors $25,258 in Past Decade

Chapter 10 Congress Has Power to Fix Social Security for Seniors

Congress agrees that CPI-W hurts the elderly; but won't do anything about it.

Like everything else for seniors, Congress is underfunding the Social Security Administration. Perhaps what's the most intriguing notion about Social Security's inflation issue is that Congress wholeheartedly agrees that seniors are getting the nasty from them and the rest of the government and the academe elite.

Democrats and Republicans agree on virtually nothing when it comes to Social Security, but both parties firmly believe that the CPI-W fails to do a good job of accurately measuring the real inflation that program beneficiaries face. Seniors are partially to blame because they just take it on the chin rather than fighting back. Seniors must speak up or they will be rewarding the very slugs in the Congress who are hurting them. I am talking about cheating seniors of over 50% of the monthly payments due them. That folks is a sin.

Unfortunately, that's where the agreement with seniors' advocates ends, and why nothing is being done about fixing Social Security's inflationary tether on Capitol Hill.

Democrats, who brought the CPI-W upon us initially, now publicly prefer replacing the CPI-W with the aforementioned CPI-E. Yet, back when they controlled the presidency and the Congress, they did not take any action to make this happen. Now that they have control again with Biden and an all-D Congress, there is not a peep at the Capitol in support of seniors. Seniors must remember this at election time or they will never recover.

In doing so, if a recalcitrant Congress ever acts together to help seniors, the belief is that COLA would expand over time since the CPI-E would do a much better job of measuring the costs that are important to seniors. But Republicans aren't in favor of using the CPI-E, which is still considered to be an experimental measure in the eyes of the BLS.

Perhaps Republicans in Congress need a few personal visits from seniors to help show Trump's coattails were never wide enough to support Republicans who may think they can get away with stiffing seniors. If I were to create a message from any President to Republicans in Congress, it would say: Give Seniors what they want and need. Do not be a *horse's ass*. Your *whinny* will give you away.

As hard as it is for me to believe, I have been told that Republicans have proposed switching from the CPI-W to the Chained CPI. If Republicans ever want to get elected again, my recommendation is to immediately back off the whole idea of a COLA that cheats seniors. The Democrats learned their lesson. Take a tip from those who now know that seniors count. Chained CPI 'R No Good!

The COLA produced by a chained-CPI would further reduce the seniors' COLA. This has not happened yet and the thinking has been around for a long while. Obama was ready to institute the Chained-CPI. Some wise advisors in BHO's administration talked the Democrat President out of using this nasty index. Republicans who like holding office must pay heed to the consequences to their future electability. My advice to all who like holding office is to Say NO to Chained CPI or forever pay the consequences. Seniors will never forgive you.

The Chained CPI takes into account the idea of substitution bias. FYI, this is a bogus way of forcing seniors to accept less COLA and getting nothing, even a smile, in return. It is the worst idea I can think of, for making right the Democrat's initial fraud in the formation of the CPI-W.

As discussed, Obama when he was president, and his Democrat advisors, were smart enough in 2014 to reject this notion. If Republicans adopt this asinine notion, they should be known ad infinitum as the Dumb Party and the Democrats should automagically become the enlightened Party. Republicans should know that time is running out to discard the Chained-CPI as even a remote possibility.

Any smart Republican who respects seniors and wants to give them back some of what was stolen from them by the Democrats needs to adopt the notion Brian Kelly puts forth in this book. Shall we call it *25 and six 5's*. That's what it is. Under the plan put forth in prior chapters, seniors would immediately receive a 25% COLA followed by a 5% above the CLI-W bump every six months for the next three years. That would get every senior off the front porch of the poorhouse and it would give any Republican candidate who had the guts to propose it, wins from now to eternity. Think about it.

Then, think about this. Whereby a consumer trades down to similar goods or services because of inflation (e.g., buying pork or chicken if ground beef prices rise), this should have no effect on the real inflation rate.

Yes, we admit that this is a real-world consumer reaction to higher prices, but no other inflationary index accounts for substitution bias as a means of punishing the ultimate consumer—the voter.

It would be dishonest not to note that switching to the Chained CPI would likely help the government's coffers and reduce the senior's COLA -- and therefore seniors' purchasing power -- even more than under the CPI-W. That's not something congressional Democrats would want to stand behind for long. If Republicans become known as the Chained CPI sponsors, their political lives will be shortened by a good measure while Democrats are laughing hard for having rejected the notion.

The Democrats so far own all the problems with CPI-W, since their minions in academe and in government have pushed the CPI-W, a mechanism to assure that seniors go further behind each year after each year.

However, if seniors spent more time working with advocates, the lily livered Republicans, fearing a voter retaliation would quickly abandon their designs for the totally fraudulent Chained CPI and would look towards something like the CPI-E and batter yet, the 25 and six 5's plan as introduced in this book.

For me, however, because of all the intentional punishment that seniors have been forced to endure over the years, even CPI-E is not enough. But, it would be an OK start with a *Seniors' Administration* pushing for the right solution

I have already revealed my plan in prior chapters. My suggestion is simply to begin a restitution process that will bring seniors back close to an "even notion." Call it reparations if you like because that is what it really is. The idea is the deal has to be sweet enough that seniors would be willing to accept, and they would soon be collecting a lot of gravy.

Consider this: Nobody seemed to care when the Democrats robbed seniors of their original well-endowed social security fund to pay everyday bills. Consequently, I refuse to entertain that seniors need to consider this in a restitution plan. The government spent seniors' dollars fraudulently and caused many seniors over the years to lose their homes. Check the records and you will find it.

My plan is to make the yearly COLA correct and very quickly. For three consecutive years, my recommendation is to suspend the calculation of the CPI-W. Instead, I would ask President Trump to order a makeup COLA of 25% plus 5% paid twice, once every six months in each of those three years.

With this process seniors would get gobs of dollars additional in their checks every six months that they should have had before being made poor by the BLS. They would even be able to get their grandkids Christmas presents again like before the BLS started to steal from them.

As a senior myself, getting such an influx of cash (25% plus 5% above the CPI-W COLA twice a year for three years) after being stiffed for so long, I would recognize that the government was ready to make it all right for seniors.

So ,after this seniors would get back a major proportion of that which was fraudulently stolen by the Democrat backed BLS and the SSA. Why not be happy if you are a senior?

Seniors would get 25% immediately and 5% increases twice a year with no calculators needed. Fire the government bureaucrat calculators and the consultant coffee breath professors in academe and use the savings to help the treasury fund the senior restitution program. That is not all that is needed, however.

Instead of any version of the CPI dash—such as -W, -U, -E, or the totally bogus dash Chained-CPI, designed to stiff seniors, the BLS should be ordered to fire 90% of their workers who had worked solely on SSR issues. They had purposely made life miserable for seniors.

The BLS organization needs to be forced to go back to the simple days of the market basket. So, after the three-years, the immediate 25% plus the twice a year 5% payment on top of the CPI calculation make-up deal, life from the BLS can go back to a better normal for seniors.

How about a real cost of living based on a real inflation rate. Who would not want that? Bring Shadowstats from the Walter John Williams organization as paid consultants for five years to set up an enduring COLA and SSR payment system that keeps seniors at or a peep ahead of the real inflation rate. n

There would be no need for any of the hocus pocus CPIs that have screwed seniors for too many years. Just use the inflation rate of 50 market basket items with the Seniors Administration doing the oversight and Shadowstats as the consultant team so the bureaucrats are never emboldened enough again to try to trick seniors out of their true cost of living bump. If necessary, let's take names.

To be sure the CPI calculation is correct without extra influence by a deep-state version of the left-behind BLS, the new honest BLS must be monitored by the Seniors Administration using easily purchasable statistics from Shadowstats. BLS and the Social Security Administration should never be without major oversight. We have seen first-hand the harm they can do.

The CPI dash nothing, which are also Shadowstats notions must be continually evaluated by fair minded presidents such as Donald Trump and after 2024, the next president and then the next, etc. The objective of course would be to assure a cybernetic system in which renegades and rogues cannot mess with the rights of seniors to receive a true inflation based COLA. The annual inflation-based increase should have nothing to do with calculations intended to diminish proper recompense.

That sounds simple does it not. The Congress could do this in an instant and the right president would sign properly written legislation. My view is that the legislation should be one or two pages or less, not more. Whichever party proposed such a bailout for seniors, in my opinion, would be in power a long time. I sure hope somebody presents this notion to Congress and the current President in the White House soon…please!

The *Medicare for all Party* that I suspect would not be in contention for many House or Senate Seats in future years, would be expected to vote against seniors. Consequently, if seniors ever want to achieve their true recompense from the government, it stands to reason that it should be many, many years for the smart

American people ever entrust their government again to goofy Democrats.

There is no doubt even in Congress today, that Social Security's COLA needs fixing. But what that fix would look like, or when it would take shape, would be anyone's guess. I sure hope my recommendation gains some weight and preference.

There is no way that the ship can make a 1940 dollar's value with real inflation the benchmark as that bird has flown away a long time ago. But the 25% immediate bump plus 5% twice a year for three years or more would at least get seniors out of the poorhouse. To make sure the proposal I outlined above ever happens, the major expediting factor would be for seniors to stop being legislation watchers, but instead become vocal. My suggestion for seniors is to schedule meetings and conferences and keep the cards and letters coming to Congress.

Social Security is a godsend to the nation's elderly but that does not mean that seniors should forgive the Congress for the fraud in the CPI-W calculation for so many years. We have proven the case already in this book. So we first need to bring most seniors out of poverty with the immediate 25% plus three years at least of 5% twice a year COLA bumps.

But that is not all. We all know that Democrats want to spend $6 trillion this year alone on pork. None of the pork, however, is intended to help seniors. It just demonstrates that there is plenty of means in government printing or whatever to create funds for "important causes" out of thin air. I would rather give it all to seniors than to have the cash go to happy pork projects for politicians.

Considering that this $6 Trillion is twice as much as what is left in Social Security's infamous trust fund, clearly a government that would take $6 Trillion for pork could afford to pay seniors back for the fraud perpetrated by not using the true value of a dollar as a yardstick over the years. There should be no measures taken such as the 24% benefits cuts because some pencil pusher thinks would be needed to save the system if the fraudulent IOUs ever go to zero.

Since most rich people make money that is of the unearned variety, they pay no SS tax on it. That needs to be fixed. How you make your money over a certain amount – say $500,000 should not matter. It should be taxed. Additionally, there should be no cap on the amount of earnings taxed for social security. These two measures alone would do wonders to bolster the SS fund by as much as $2 Trillion per year.

The other idea never discussed is that the government has stolen much of what would be much larger current payments from SSR recipients by not calculating a fair cost of goods (inflation). So, seniors are due a ton of money from the government which actually still cheats seniors by shortchanging their COLA each year.

Whenever the mythical fund, stuffed with un-collectible IOUs (Federal Treasury Notes) gets to zero, the payments to seniors should not be reduced. Instead, the checks should come out of the general fund and it would take at least 100 years for the government to pay back seniors for what it has stolen from them. Let the government figure out how to get the funds to pay back seniors. Seniors should not pay to have seniors reconstituted. That makes no sense.

I am also for means-testing Social security benefits. My dad always said social security is for retirement with dignity. But if means testing ever is determined to be the best way to collect welfare payments from the rich then Chris Christie, when he was a presidential candidate, did outline one of the best and simplest plans I have seen.

Before we get to that let's consider that the most an individual who files a claim for Social Security retirement benefits in 2021 can receive per month is: $3,895 for someone who files at age 70; $3,148 for someone who files at full retirement age (currently 66 and 2 months); and thirdly, $2,324 for someone who files at 62.

My suggestion before we get into Christie's is that we encourage rich people to quietly and not publicly donate their SSR checks to the SSR fund. Let's leave it at that.

We know that even the richest Americans can qualify for Social Security retirement benefits. Even though they don't need the extra income, social security is not a welfare plan and seniors do not want to receive welfare from anybody unless they need it.

Billionaires and less can qualify for Social Security benefits when they reach age 62, and many of the richest Americans are currently collecting a monthly Social Security check that they really do not need for sustenance. I think it would be good for government to create a compelling argument for these people to donate their SSR back to the SSR fund. It is that simple.

If we ever decided to make Social Security (SS) a welfare program and I would be against it because there are better ways, the Christie plan is simple as a way to save dollars for the sustenance of the IOU fund. Here is what Christie said:

"I propose a modest means test that only affects those with non-Social Security income of over $80,000 per year, and phases out Social Security payments entirely for those that have $200,000 a year of other income." He also added the qualification that these proposals would not apply to people who are currently old—if you are already collecting in other words, you would continue to collect.

IMAGE SOURCE: GETTY IMAGES.

Raise the income cap for SSR

Among the many ideas put on the table to strengthen Social Security, none has garnered more popularity with the American public (via surveys) than raising or eliminating the maximum taxable earnings cap associated with the payroll tax.

Social Security's 12.4% payroll tax on earned income is unquestionably the program's funding workhorse. In 2019, almost $945 billion of the $1.06 trillion collected was derived from the payroll tax. Take note that while the self-employed are responsible for the full 12.4% tax, workers employed by a company or someone else split this payroll tax liability with their employer. Thus, most workers only pay 6.2% of their earned income into Social Security, with their employer also covering a 6.2% share.

The catch is that the payroll tax only applies to earned income (that's wages and salary, but not investment income) between $0.01 and $137,700, as of 2020. This $137,700 figure is what's known as the maximum taxable earnings cap.

The year-over-year percentage increase in the National Average Wage Index dictates how much the tax cap will rise each year.

Approximately 94% of working Americans won't earn $137,700 in wages or salary this year, which means they'll be paying into Social Security with every dollar they make.

Comparatively, the roughly 6% of workers who will top $137,700 will see a portion, or perhaps the majority, of their income exempted from the payroll tax. Between 1983 and 2016, the amount of earnings exempted from the payroll tax roughly quadrupled from north of $300 billion to $1.2 trillion. That is a lot of sheckles.

Thus, raising or eliminating the payroll tax cap is a means of taxing well-to-do workers in order to generate additional income for Social Security.

I would like to help others run for Congress. I hope they would want to be fair and honest. I think all seniors should send in their cards and letters. To me, a lot of impact would be if a constituent said they had had enough and were ready to write about running for Congress themselves in a nicely penned letter to the editor in the home town paper.

Many of the ideas in this chapter were mostly the work of Sean Williams from Motley Fool.

Chapter 11 Boost Social Security Right Now!

Why is Social Security a taboo to discuss in political campaigns?

After the last several chapters, you might expect this coming. There is only one major reason why we can no longer talk about this serious issue in America. Democrats no longer have a love affair with seniors. Funny how they forgot that they did not come from eggs. Like God, Trump, and Trump Supporters, seniors have become unloved in Democrat circles, where there is no free speech on any topic permitted, Social Security is an especially heinous topic.

Why? Because Democrats are not interested in making life better for a group of stubborn old farts who are dead set against Marxism, socialism, communism, liberalism, and progressivism. Seniors are for life, liberty, and the pursuit of happiness.

When last did you hear anybody talking about Social Security who was not bragging about the great 1.6% that our benevolent government just "given" to seniors?" It is 5.9% this year but Medicare increases ate up half of that and inflation itself at 10% nowadays has eaten up just about the rest. Seniors are negative again. It is a shame and a disgrace for our government to treat seniors so shabbily. If it were not the government as the perpetrator, it would be a prosecutable crime. It should be.

Each year, as we have already learned, seniors lose more spending power. Social Security topics are simply not permitted even in Democrat free-speech zones as politicos do not want seniors to know about the major Democrat sponsored rip-off with government bureaucrats and coffee-breath professors in academe. Remember the biggest boss in the Democrat Party of today, Barack Obama, first blessed the notion of giving zero COLA or close to zero during his presidency. How is that for a great Democrat legacy?

Consequently, it is no longer publicly discussed nor is it a topic in newspaper articles by our duplicitous media, despite the fact that seniors' issues need the spotlight now more than ever. Of course every Democrat candidate is using the time-tested "D" liars playbook which includes scare tactics to intimidate seniors about losing everything. Can't you see Granny getting pushed off a cliff as I say this. Yet, like most everything spun by Democrats today including memories of Trump's impeachment, even the Granny tale is a big lie.

Part of the leftist's playbook is the big lie. Thus, today's Marxists, socialists, communists, liberals, and progressives are all part of the Liars Party. We'll all live better lives if we remember that. Remember who started the big CPI-rip-off—Democrats.

Republicans have recognized the importance of seniors for a long time before the 2000 presidential election. In 2016, Republicans found that 53 percent of adults 65 and older voted for President Donald Trump. Trump campaigned on protecting Medicare and Social Security and lowering drug prices. Democrats under

President Obama concentrated on lowering the COLA to save the government money.

Let me repeat for old time sake. This is the same dishonest Democrat Party that was throwing Granny off the cliff just a few years ago. Now, they simply point at their candidate's opponent and they say that he or she wants to lower Social Security—even though it is not true. Only a fool would want to do that, but Democrats know that play has worked in every election because Democrats deep down want to believe their own big lie.

The Democrat-controlled media helps the Party in all of its bidding. For example, they suggest that seniors are greedy. In unison, they deride the implied greed of SSR recipients who received a whopping .1.6 percent cost of living raise to kick off 2020.

Democrats are obviously oblivious to the fact that the real inflation rate from October 2018 to October 2019 was a real 6 percent (not 1.6%) using Walter "John" Williams' Shadowstats and about 9% using Ed Butowsky's Chapwood Index. We have discussed both alternate inflation indexes in proper chapters but these indices will be explained in detail shortly.

They both give Democrats a bad grade on preserving seniors' standard of living. The more seniors hear about these alternatives, the better they can appreciate the big scandal perpetrated by the government for the last 36-yars and even more by our once trustworthy government.

The point for seniors is that real inflation rate is anywhere from 6% to 9% (splitting the difference of Chapwood and Shadowstats at 7.5%). Seniors in essence paid 6% to 9% more in the last year than the prior year for the same goods and services. Meanwhile the totally fraudulent, government created CPI-W, which as noted is a group effort of coffee breath professors in academe and frustrated Democrat government analysts says that even though seniors paid 7.5% more, they should get just 20% of that—a measly 1.6% COLA.

More and more seniors facing such differences of reality v the fake CPI-W each year are being forced to move into small studio apartments from their long-time family homes—if they can even afford the rental costs. Some give up, pack it up, and sign up for welfare housing as a way to survive.

No wonder seniors are struggling when their cost for purchases goes up 7.5% and their COLA to make up for that is a mere 1.6% These are 2019 cost of living figures that affected seniors in 2020. How do I know that, and most don't? It is not popular for Democrats to tell the truth or to provide any facts when they implicate the Party in the travesty.

The government got even more aggressive in stiffing seniors in October 2020 announcing the "generous" 1.3% COLA that we "enjoyed" last year. Meanwhile as you can see in the calculator below, the real inflation rate was 9%:

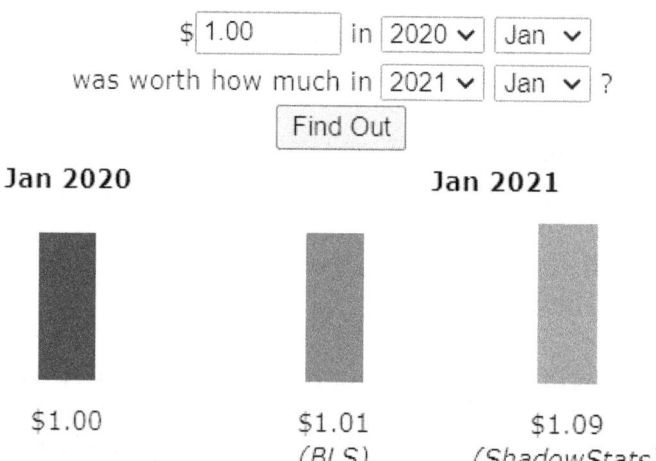

BLS: Bureau of Labor Statistics, CPI-U
ShadowStats: Shadow Government Statistics Alternate CPI.

By the way, if Obama had his way with an even more unfair Chained CPI, a contrivance he supported against his advisor's wishes during his second term, it would be even worse. Seniors all know that the former president gave zero cost increases three times during his presidency and almost zero (0.3%) one other time. This clearly shows the Democrats' lack-of-love for seniors.

In 2014, the president pushed hard for advancing a surreptitious continual reduction of Social Security benefits by using the fraudulent Chained-CPI mechanism. Obama's dubious market calculations would have cost retirees more than 2 percent of their incomes. The Chained-CPI is a Democrat innovation. Yet, today all Democrats are blaming the Chained CPI on Republicans. That of course is a lie but try to get a Democrat to believe that it is not true.

There are several ways senior Americans can investigate how much government lies cost them each year. The government purposely underestimates the cost of living using CPI-W or chained CPI to deprive the elderly of a commensurate actual increase in earned benefits. One such method for you to use to calculate your personal loss to government fraud each year is to subscribe to the Chapwood index or you may explore Shadowstats.com. In these sources there is proof-a-plenty, and the information is not government propaganda.

Seniors unfortunately are running out of whatever financial cushions they may ever have had, and their plight today is dire. I encourage you all to research the degree to which government deceptions are resulting in these surreptitious deprivations.

The Chapwood Index
http://www.chapwoodindex.com/

After decades of Americans being saturated by our mainstream propaganda rags, it is refreshing to finally see the truth in print. The Chapwood Index reflects the true cost-of-living increase in America. It is updated and released twice a year. There, the ruses or mis-directions by the government are not included in its pages. Instead, it truthfully reports the unadjusted actual cost and price fluctuation of the top 500 items on which Americans spend their after-tax dollars in the 50 largest cities in the nation.

It exposes why middle-class Americans—salaried workers who are given routine pay hikes and retirees who depend on annual increases in their corporate pension and Social Security payments—cannot maintain their standard of living. Plainly and simply, the Index shows that their income can't keep up with their expenses and it explains why they increasingly have to turn to the government for entitlements for supplementation.

Mainstream Democrats such as Joe Biden, Nancy Pelosi, Maxine Waters, and Chuck Schumer exacerbate the situation by allowing the use of even more inequitable methods such as the new chained CPI to help assure that seniors can languish in poverty as soon as possible. Clearly and unfortunately, President Biden though he beats the Democratic Drum incessantly, does not understand what he is doing. e

The problem of lacking transparency on true costs (true inflation) occurs because salary and benefit increases are pegged to the fraudulent Consumer Price Index (CPI), which for more than a century has purported to reflect the fluctuation in prices for a typical "basket of goods" in American cities — but which actually hasn't done that for a more than the last 36 years.

The middle class has seen its purchasing power decline dramatically in the last three+ decades, forcing more and more people to seek entitlements when their savings are gone. And as long as pay raises and benefit increases are tied to a false CPI, this trend sees no end.

How many of your friends have said there is no inflation? None, I bet! How can they say there is no inflation when we all see it in our insurance premiums, at the gas pump, in the supermarket, and in medical and health costs—yes, just about everything. Are we to believe that our government lives on a different planet? Or, are they simply lying?

In the past, nobody was anxious to throw the proverbial grandma under the bus. Now, believe it or not, hordes of constituencies are lining up to be the first to fleece what should belong to her, into the eternal abyss, never to be seen again.

The list of offenders includes: Congress, government officials, professors in academia, and the "greatest" economic advisors the world has ever known. Besides all these frauds, we must add the dejected stand-alone CPI-W economists who cannot gain tenure at any university.

This group of elite misfits have formed a diabolical consortium to cheat seniors out of their due cost of living increases promised from the very day the SSR act was passed in 1935 by Franklin Delano Roosevelt.

Roosevelt Signs Social Security Act of 1935. August 14, 1935. The Social Security Act (H.R. 7260, Public Law No. 271, 74th Congress) became law with the President's signature at approximately 3:30 p.m. on a Wednesday.

Admittedly, the Democrats with a Democrat President, Franklin D. Roosevelt, brought Social Security into being. Yet, there is good reason to believe that it was also the Democrats who raided social security to beef up the treasury. Surely somebody knows the real answer but for some reason, nobody can say definitively what really happened to the massive amount of funds that once were there except they are gone.

Americans believe that a Democratic Congress stole SSR funds from Social Security?

As most Americans understand, for its 80-plus years, Social Security has been a financial rock for our nation's elderly. In recent years, three of five elderly Americans get a portion of their sustenance from the Social Security Fund. Unlike welfare, which was enacted by Congress to take dollars from the treasury to give to those deemed needy, Social Security is not an entitlement. It is contributory.

The system was set up so that most Americans would earn themselves a retirement benefit by working hard for decades before they were permitted to retire with dignity and begin collecting their due pension from what was then a huge Social Security Fund.

The idea is that when seniors do hang up their work gloves for good, there's a good chance they'll be collecting in some form from Social Security. Of the 60% leaning on the program, they will be receiving about half of their income from reliance on Social Security in some capacity to make ends meet. It is what it is.

Americans would have to be living in Space or the Twilight Zone to not have been introduced to the fact that the program is facing hardships like never before. The biggest challenge since its inception, according to the Board of Trustees report is that this important program now expends more than it collects in revenue each year.

How Social Security got into this bind is often a source of contentious debate. However, one avenue of blame almost always leads to the Lyndon B. Johnson administration.

Did President Johnson Steal SSR Funds?

Back in 1968, President Johnson made a change to the presentation of the federal budget, choosing to include Social Security and its trust funds. This created what was known then as the "unified budget." With this, many economists found that there was a good chance that SSR funds were mixed with regular treasury funds to handle big expenses such as the Vietnam War and the War on Poverty.

1969, the height of the Vietnam War was the first year that Social Security and its trust funds were presented "on-budget" with all federal spending.

Americans believe Congress raided SSR

We'd be lying if we suggested that Americans think Congress has managed the Social Security Funds judiciously. Quite the opposite. A big concern among many Americans is that the Democrat tinkering with on-budget and off-budget approaches while juggling huge SSR balances permitted the federal government to comingle funds from Social Security's trusts and net cash surpluses with general government spending.

In essence, there's the strong belief that Congress raided the Social Security trust funds to finance government activities, ranging from education and healthcare to the ongoing Vietnam War. Do you trust the government? Think about while you read the rest of this book.

To be more specific about the SSR cash fund story we have discussed, the rest of the story is that they're currently loaned out to the federal government, as required by law. Yes, the treasury does get its hands on SSR cash—all $2.9 trillion of it that has been built up since its inception. It is not sitting in a vault collecting dust.

Instead, the Feds are using it. They borrowed this money by selling the Social Security Administration (SSA) special-issue bonds, and they do use it to fund various line items in its general budget. Some folks strongly believe that if the federal government paid back what it has borrowed, with interest, Social Security would be just fine and not facing any long-term problems. Do you trust your government?

Government bureaucrats call this wishful thinking. I find it very plausible and it would take an awful lot for me to believe the central government is not responsible for any shortfall that may be projected. Seniors should not ever be forced to pony up to make up for what the feds stole from Social Security.

As the mainstream Democrats kowtow to cultural elites and financial institutions, turning their backs on the workers and middle-class that defined their constituency for much of the 20th century, it is up to us to pick up the slack and fight for the rights of everyday Americans. We cannot afford to trust the treasury department to do it for us.

When SSR was enacted, the president promised full dollar value throughout the years in order to ensure its passage in 1935. We cannot let this be undermined by the likes of Chuck Schumer and Nancy Pelosi.

Many Americans are concerned that the Social Security program itself may not be able to sustain itself while others see the government cheating on the cost of living increases (CPI) thereby predetermining a life of squalor for seniors.

All successful societies throughout the ages, have maintained respect and dignity for their elders. Not only is cheating seniors a moral failure, it is a sign of a civilization entering an era of decay.

While seniors are losing their homes and many, for want of bread and milk, are on the verge of heading to the proverbial poorhouse or worse—the clutches of the Grim Reaper, Congress in 2018 pretended to care, giving a 2% raise, but then quickly snatched it right back in the dead of night via a Medicare Part B premium increase.

This additional Medicare Part B charge for necessary health services for seniors was excluded from the cost of living calculations. How could Congress have missed that? They pulled a repeat performance last year again for 2020 yet it was worse—just 1.3%.

Thus, to pay Medicare part B, seniors were forced in this past year, to use their "generous" 2% raises, rather than to offset the costs brought forth from inflation for which the 2% was intended. Since the real inflationary cost increases were closer to 11% using the popular non-government indexes, that means that instead of 9% that seniors were to endure, they accrued a full load of 11% in price increases.

It's easy to understand why this constant drainage of resources is unsustainable for a senior citizen. More and more are forced to go to welfare or give up as their homes are foreclosed.

Some suggest that seniors were sold a risk-free retirement with Social Security. Now they face foreclosure. Urban African American neighborhoods are hardest hit as nearly 100,000 loans have failed. Yes, after the great recession, nearly 100,000 loans that allowed senior citizens to tap into their home equity have failed, blindsiding elderly borrowers and their families and dragging down property values in their neighborhoods.

In many cases, the worst toll has fallen on those ill-equipped to shoulder it—urban African Americans, many of whom worked for most of their lives, then found themselves struggling in retirement. Today's elderly homeowners were often wooed into borrowing money through special programs designed to rip off their meager savings in equity.

Way too many endured and fell for attractive sales pitches or it was their dire need for cash – or both. When they missed a paperwork deadline or fell behind on taxes or insurance, lenders moved swiftly to foreclose on the home. Those foreclosures could have been avoided if the CPI would have been calculated fairly. But instead, their savings were wiped out and tough times wiped out hard-earned generational wealth built.

It should not have been and the immediate 25% plus six 5% bumps above the CPI are designed to get it back on track and no more foreclosures—no more poorhouse.

It is my contention that Congress must pay this back to seniors. There is a lot owed. Even the 25% immediate payment plus three years of semi-annual 5% COLA bumps (6 in total) as I recommend will not pay back seniors all of what has been stolen and thus what is owed. However, it will place seniors on a positive road to the future.

After the first three years, the payback period would be over. Then, real market basket price inflation must then be used to calculate COLA—no more estimates. This is money owed to seniors. It is not a gift or welfare of any kind. It should have no impact on the government's ability to create a way to fund social security for the long haul

Think about it. The big argument against the SSR fund ever going bankrupt is that Congress would never allow a huge cut to Social Security benefits in light of the program's popularity and the importance of benefits. Even if the trust fund were to run dry, lawmakers would simply make up the difference out of general revenue. We know that. They are politicians.

Why has Congress not fixed the CPI-W problem?

Given the fact that almost every analyst knows Congress would not permit the impact of a cut in SSR benefits, how can Congress give 1.6%. When the cost of living is really 6% or more, how has Congress gotten away with giving 1.6%? It is simple. *Subterfuge.*

Most seniors do not know they are being stiffed. That's why I wrote this book?

Picture government bureaucrats and coffee breath professors from academe as consultants. They go into a room with the objective being to stiff seniors and add dollars to the general fund. They dust off the prior year's methodology and figure out how to take a few extra bucks for Uncle Sam. They agree that their numbers are good and then; they set a low expectation level with some leaks and finally announce an almost zero number and call it the new CPI-W for the next year. That's what we see. It is all lies.

I regret to say that this method of continual lying is very effective and was used by Germany in its darkest days during the big War. Here is the methodology used by Wartime Minister of Propaganda in Germany, Joseph Goebbels. It is very scary. Our own government now is using this method and that makes it even scarier:

Think about this. "If you tell a lie big enough and keep repeating it, people will eventually come to believe it. The lie can be maintained only for such time as the State can shield the people from the political, economic and /or military consequences of the lie. It thus becomes vitally important for the State to use all of its powers to repress dissent, for the truth is the mortal enemy of the lie, and thus by extension, the truth is the greatest enemy of the State. Think a little longer. Is this what you see?

Last year their number was 1.6 % while Shadowstats says true inflation was approximately 6% while the Chapwood Index said it was over 9%. And, so the CPI-W is a rip-off for seniors of 500% to 700% and our government is not open about it.

They instead pretend and lie about their calculations being truthful but we know they are not. My one-time adjustment over three years and then using the real cost of living will solve this problem forever as long as we have a Seniors Administration assuring that the government stays honest.

To repeat the solution, seniors would get 10% COLA for three straight years, twice a year. So, after six, six-month COLAs, followed by receiving the true inflation rate as an annual cola after the third year, life for seniors would be better. All of the government bureaucrats in the BLS hoax and their coffee-breath assistants in academe could be laid off or fired.

And, so, to repeat, from year four onward, the *actual inflation rate*, not the CPI-W, CPI-U, CPI-E, or the Chained CPI would be used henceforth to calculate a proper COLA for each senior's payment to be of constant value from year to year.

How did we reach this point?

Early in the administration of disgraced former Democrat President Bill Clinton, an economist named Michael Boskin, and Alan Greenspan, Chairman of the Board of Governors of the Federal Reserve System, devised a scheme that would allow for market basket "substitutions" to artificially lower the cost of living and result in lower payments to our oldest Americans. It was a scheme to purposely stiff seniors from ever achieving a true cost of living COLA again.

These guys found value in having senior citizens help save the big government money. Prior to their involvement, the consumer price index (CPI) was measured using the cost of a fixed basket of goods, a fairly simple and straightforward concept.

The identical basket of goods would be priced at prevailing market costs for each period, and the period-to-period change in the cost of that market basket represented the rate of inflation in terms of maintaining a constant standard of living. That was self-evidently fair and reasonable, and predictably resulted in seniors receiving annual COLA increases in tandem with the prices of goods actually increasing.

But Boskin and Alan Greenspan argued that when one item in the basket, for instance steak, became too expensive, the consumer would substitute hamburger for the steak, and that the inflation measure should reflect the costs tied to buying hamburger rather than the steak. Eventually, it became OK for the bureaucrats to replace hamburger with less expensive tuna and eventually because the protein value was the same, the price of cat tuna replaced regular tuna in the market basket.

The Bureaucrats like to tell observers that seniors did not have to eat the cat tuna, but their basket costs would be the same if they did.

In simple terms, the government began to play games with Social Security's annual inflation adjustments. It was intentional. To further obscure the true cost of living, other items were selectively removed from the basket when the prices were high and then reinserted when the prices were low. The objective was to save the government money--not to make sure that things were fair for elderly Americans. Shame on the bureaucrats!

Over the years, many people have been familiar with this ruse. For example, an economic commentator named Barry Ritholtz joked that Greenspan's core inflation metric can more accurately be described as "inflation ex-inflation," meaning inflation after all of the inflation has been excluded. This demonstrates that the deception of seniors has been intentional, and it continues with a new notion called the chained CPI that would cost seniors even more. We need a president and a Congress to get this back on track.

The fact is that government has deceitfully stolen directly from the pockets of our beloved seniors by denying them a fair cost of living increase—just to stay even. Some have even suggested that the government believes a natural limit exists so they won't get caught in their ruse. They think they will get no criticism because over time, many of the complainants will be silenced by their deaths when they can no longer afford to pay up. Charming thought?

Walter J. Williams, an American blessing who operates the Shadowstats site, and whose article is in Chapter 8 of this book, demonstrates every day on his web site that seniors have been stiffed by much more than just 125% and in fact should be receiving more than 4 times what their dollars were worth in 1980. That's $450 instead of $100.00.

Any senior would love to have even a small proportion of that loss back. Government lies cost $350.00 since 1980. But nobody will ever see that and even great representatives, are not telling Americans that it is happening. They lie even to their loyal constituents.

I hope I have convinced you all that seniors have been ripped off and are being ripped off financially all the time by their own government. Congress is the real culprit.

A gradual remedy for seniors, since it would be difficult to give seniors the proper increase immediately needed to offset this total quagmire caused by government malfeasance over many years, my recommendation would be to approach it gradually, in a way that seniors would be somewhat pleased, and be able to live out their golden years in a much more dignified manner. Who can argue with that?

In this chapter, I show how this is to be achieved. As noted, Seniors would be much better off after receiving a 25% immediate payment followed by 5% above CPI-W CoLA six times in three years and then for the rest of their lives seniors would receive a COLA like in the olden days—reflecting the true cost of inflation. After three consecutive years with seven CoLA boosts, that should be sufficient to remove seniors from the on-deck circle they currently occupy directly outside the homeless shelter.

That's all it would take. Then we can use the measurements that were in effect before the government fraud, in which a dollar was a dollar and a dime was a dime, and the US must vow to never stiff seniors again.

Thank you, dear readers, for your attention on these important matters.

In conclusion, I must again express my gratitude for your consideration and any support as we work together to make America even greater. God bless America and help us all make her better!

An Alternative

Seniors know they have been stiffed big-time because of indices such as Shadowstats and Chapwood. As we introduced several times in recent chapters, and will continue to expound upon as we progress, I ask you to remember the name *"The Chapwood Index."* It is but one of a number of truthful alternative determinations of the real inflation rate without requiring the reader to hold a PhD in economics. Shadowstats is the best and most accurate inflation index.

Chapter 12 Hey Buddy; Can You Spare a Dime?

A group of senior citizens march through New York City in 1961, trying to urge the Kennedy administration to add health care coverage to Social Security. Four years later, Social Security was amended to include the transformative programs Medicaid and Medicare. Harry Harris/AP

SSR Benefits Raise 2018/2019 was a net of zero

FYI, there is no official abbreviation for social security or social security retirement. Therefore, in this book as noted previously, we choose to use our own abbreviation *SSR* to mean social security as well as for social security retirement. As many know, the German Army in World War II commandeered the term SS and, so we will stay far away from any negative connotation by staying away from that abbreviation. Think *SSR* for S̲ocial S̲ecurity R̲etirement.

When President Trump was inaugurated in 2017, the paltry increase from President Obama's last year in office was 0.3%. That is .003 for those like me who want to really know where the decimal point is. It was the smallest non-zero COLA ever given and many wondered if Obama felt he could really afford it. What a miser.

I don't think that President Trump intended to slam seniors like Obama did; but they got slammed nonetheless. Obama's last approved COLA increment was implemented by the newly elected President Trump. Seniors who think this President does no wrong are now hoping he sees what happened throughout the Obama years and about thirty-six years before, and that he adjusts things retroactively soon to where they should be awful close to being correct. No senior should have to miss a wholesome meal because their government has cheated them.

The potential benefits increase for millions of seniors in 2018 for 2019 was expected to be larger than usual to make up for the past abuses by government in calculating the inflation rate. After Obama's almost-zero last rate at 0.3%, President Trump's announced the rate at 2%. Admittedly this was about six times more than the 4 bucks (.03%) raise per month in Obama's swan-song last year .

But it still did not make up for the actual inflation rate's impact on seniors' income. President Trump did not focus on seniors as he had a big mess to clean up plus Democrats were making it difficult all the while for him during his tenure as our president. He was wrongly impeached twice during his one term in office . He had little time to do much else than defend himself. Yet, the Trump policies that Biden cast into the garbage can in January 2021, as we all know by now were very wise and helpful to America and Americans. Don't we all miss having a great brave and intelligent president to lead our land?

The miniscule amount of COLA did nothing to counteract the intentional lowball CPI official inflation rates, endured for over thirty-six years by seniors. There was a time thirty-six years ago when SSR monthly payments were large enough for seniors to catch up to the cost of living. No longer!

The plan for an immediate 25% followed by three years of semiannual 5% bumps above the CPI-W rate, as noted previously brings seniors back to about as much as we could get at one time. Let's hope somebody implements that plan soon. Over the years, Government ineptness and no oversight, permitted these payments to lose their value and this cost seniors many thousands of dollars.

Despite this act being fraudulent, the Congress is not naïve. They knew exactly what they had done.

In government, the left hand takes what the right hand gives. Seniors had already gotten the bad news early that Medicare premiums for physicians' services rose again in 2017 and in 2018, 19, and 20, it happened again. Even when 2019 was almost over, seniors learned they were getting whacked again The Medicare Part-B increase again consumed the entire cost-of-living adjustment for most seniors.

The same government that thinks seniors should get 2% to help with increased costs and out of pocket expenses, stole back its 2%. Thus none of the higher costs caused by real inflation were mitigated. Seniors lost again. Hey Buddy, Can You Spare A Dime?

Brother, Can You Spare a Dime? is a 1975 documentary film starring Walt Disney, Bing Crosby, Charlie Chaplin, Andrews Sisters, Fred Astaire, Shirley Temple, Eleanor Roosevelt, and Franklin Delano Roosevelt. It was produced by Image Entertainment, consisting largely of newsreel footage and contemporary film clips to portray the era of the Great Depression and the tough times experienced equally by most Americans.

The BLS and their miserly COLA have brought hard times such as those reflected above on today's seniors. It must be fixed ASAP.

"Brother, Can You Spare A Dime?"

They used to tell me I was building a dream
And so I followed the mob
When there was earth to plow or guns to bear
I was always there, right on the job

They used to tell me I was building a dream
With peace and glory ahead
Why should I be standing in line
Just waiting for bread?

Once I built a railroad, I made it run
Made it race against time
Once I built a railroad, now it's done
Brother, can you spare a dime?

Once I built a tower up to the sun
Brick and rivet and lime
Once I built a tower, now it's done
Brother, can you spare a dime?

Once in khaki suits, gee, we looked swell
Full of that Yankee Doodly Dum
Half a million boots went slogging through Hell
And I was the kid with the drum

Chapter 12 Hey Buddy; Can You Spare a Dime?

Say, don't you remember? They called me 'Al'
It was 'Al' all the time
Why don't you remember? I'm your pal
Say buddy, can you spare a dime?

Once in khaki suits, ah, gee, we looked swell
Full of that Yankee Doodly Dum
Half a million boots went slogging through Hell
And I was the kid with the drum

Oh, say, don't you remember? They called me 'Al'
It was 'Al' all the time
Say, don't you remember? I'm your pal
Buddy, can you spare a dime?

To the rest of the Country, the Trump era was the bringing in of prosperity that had been absent for at least eight years. But, as we have pointed out in this book, not everybody was gaining. Seniors are still suffering just as in the Obama years as they work through the Great CPI Depression, with its major inflation tax. So far, there is no recovery in sight for seniors. Now that Trump is gone and Biden is in charge, there is little hope for seniors for the next four years. Our only chance is if somebody close to Biden reads this book and knows how to speak code to the current president. It is probably too much to ask to hope that Biden will know it is time for the Seniors Administration.

With what the Congress has done to seniors over the last thirty-six years, you could legitimately swear that every Congressman in Washington is either an Ostrich or a buffoon. They have their heads so far into the sand that they can actually say they do not know what they are doing to seniors. But, it has been going on for so long, seniors know they know. It is time to send them home when elections are fair again.

Among other things to cheat seniors, the legislators know that the healthcare costs for a teenager is lots less than for a senior. Nonetheless, the part of CPI for healthcare is just a bit over 6%. But it costs seniors 25% of their checks. Try buying a few Lipitor pills on that. Healthcare insurance costs have gotten out of hand, they must be put back into the cost of living formulas.

Seniors 65 and older spend more than twice as much on health care, and those 75 and older spend nearly three times more on health care than younger consumers. Congress ignores their plight. I am asking our president to address this by putting healthcare into the cost of living as it should be. First, of course the payback of an immediate 25% and 5% above CPI-W twice a year for three years must be effected. The new Seniors Administration when and of course, if, it gets here needs to be the focus for the reset.

Not only do health care expenditures steadily increase with age but health care costs have also consistently risen much faster than other market basket categories. The current price index known technically as CPI-W, does not take these critical differences in the elderly population into consideration.

Maybe the old white guys in Congress do not need their SSR pensions but they take them anyway. Maybe they have so much money they do not notice but if SSR was all they had, like most seniors, they'd notice right away. Seniors under this US government for the past 36 years are lucky if they can eat a nutritious meal every day that their Lipitor supply is low.

I can see no reason why the Congress does not know the perilous predicament in which they place seniors by their lack of support for senior issues. At election time, other than the Democrats saying Republicans are going to take it all away—all SSR, there is no candidate talking about the fraud, well known to Congress, that keeps seniors in the poorhouse and then locks the door to recovery. We need the President to change this ASAP. Tell the President about the Brian Kelly Senior Recompense (Restitution Plan) and hopefully, he will be moved to fix the problem.

Congress is smart enough to know yet it chooses not to act. They know that seniors spend a significant portion of their income on out-of-pocket health care expenses not covered by Medicare. As time goes by, each and every year, they also know that more and more of their Social Security benefit checks are eaten up and will continue to be eaten up at a higher rate by rising health care costs and a failure to acknowledge the true inflation rate.

According to the Medicare Trustees, 33 percent of the average senior's Social Security check will be consumed by Medicare out-of-pocket costs. Today the number is already 25 percent. Yet, the 25 percent is not part of the CPI and so this past year's 2% increase did not help pay for increased health care costs. That is simply not fair unless the government creates a government pharmacy and begins to give away medication.

If it were possible, I would suggest for seniors to elect their own Congresspersons because today, there is nobody in Congress, or so it seems who is watching out for our oldest generation—our parents, grandparents and great grandparents. They know but when confronted with facts about the plight of seniors, they put their heads deeper in the sand.

The truth is that if a candidate for the House or the Senate offered to solve the fraudulent CPI problem for seniors, and promise to create a Seniors Administration, they would get almost every senior vote. Any takers out there? Somebody please tell President the next presidential candidate that it is a sure way to achieve election.

Chapter 13 More Proof—System Is Rigged

Some sources calculate cost of living perfectly

Government chooses not to use the true cost of inflation. They know what it is but choose not to use it for the SSR CoLA. I just took a run out to a great site that knows that the government is corrupt on the CPI and that its corruption is far-reaching, and it harms seniors every day. There are other references to ShadowStats in this book and they all are positive for seniors.

Shadowstats.com is a web site that has been run by Walter "John" Williams for years. Williams figured out something that the government does not want you or I to know about. Don't take notes on this book, as his web site is all you need plus the references in this book's chapters will provide great reading in which you will better understand why and how Shadowstats.com can calculate an accurate rate of inflation.

You have also learned that the people that we the people pay to do the same thing for the government cannot get it done accurately. The US government bureaucrats with help from coffee-breath professors on contract from academe cannot come up with hardly anything that is accurate. Not only that but they are fine with their intentional miscalculations.

The Consumer Price Index (CPI) as calculated by the US Bureau of Labor Statistics (BLS). It is manipulated intentionally to produce a lower number than actual so seniors will be denied their proper benefits increases year after year. These increases, for those that think seniors are getting raises, are merely brought forth to keep seniors *even* with inflation. There are no bonuses for seniors in the formula. In fact they are calculated to cost seniors a few percentage points less on their payments each year. ,

When government cheats on the calculations, seniors lose purchasing power. Some cannot afford to eat; cannot afford their medicine; and others get so down in debt that they see their homes foreclosed.

The choir already should be echoing OOOOH OOOOH—whatever, that sounds like as the government calculated CPI, regardless of its suffix is—a sham. Maybe it does not matter if only old people are being "screwed."

Government lies all the time and Obama loved to lie the most about his fake-CPI equating to the cost of living for seniors because it (what's that name for a respectable term for "screwed") them. It never did get it right. It always missed the mark. We all now know that it was intentional.

The government lies were effective v seniors as they accomplished their mission. They helped the US government—our government— save treasury dollars by cheating all seniors out of their appropriate cost of living increases for years and years—at least thirty-six of them.

Chapter 13 More Proof That the System Is Rigged   143

Inflation Calculator

$ [100]   in [1975 ▼] [Jul ▼]
was worth how much in [2021 ▼] [Jul ▼] ?
[Find Out]

Jul 1975   Jul 2021

$100.00 $503.70 $3637.39
                      (BLS)   (ShadowStats)

BLS: Bureau of Labor Statistics, CPI-U
ShadowStats: Shadow Government Statistics Alternate CPI.

Please take the time to examine the chart above so I am able to make my point about the extent of the US government lies with real statistics. We can all agree that I have some 2021 and 2022 statistics in the book but some examples are a bit older. Please indulge me that the ShadowStats example above demonstrates well but it is about a year old. Look at it closely, please.

Look at the line in the figure where it says *(ShadowStats)* in parenthesis under the vertical green bar. Color can be seen in Kindle book versions but not in hard copy. It is under the words, *Jul 2021*

This 100% accurate information produced by Walter "John: Williams by the way is not provided for free, but it is available and that is very good. Williams' information is available on subscription and I bought a subscription to use for this book. I hope that it is used by the current administration to correct the lies and make the correct reparation payments to the seniors who are still alive. Would somebody please tell Biden about this? I will send him a complimentary copy of this book.

Also on that same "line," you can see when you look really hard that to get this calculator to show the 46-year inflation value from 1975 through 2015, I typed in $100.00 for the value of the money in 1975. The CPI total of $503.70 is the amount that $100 was worth in August 2015 about forty six years later. The value of money never stands still. This is about a 500% difference. The government bureaucrats and the coffee-breath professors under contract, cost seniors at least this much as they committed fraud that was OK's by the US government. 3679.39 is how much the real inflation rate would make that same $100.00 over 36 times more value.

Take the same dime that in 1975 might get you into the local movie theatre and see if they will let you in today. Try to buy a big bag of chips or popcorn for a nickel. Now, you have the idea. The purchasing power of that dime in 1975 was a dime. But the same purchasing power of the dime invested at the true inflation rate is about 50 cents. In my world this is about 5 times the value if 1975 is the year in question. Yet, seniors are not frolicking in such a 500% increase in benefits, which should be called a break-even.

Why not? Government lies… that's why!

I hope that the current president sees these stats and says to his team: "Brian Kelly is right. Even if I give a 25% immediate bump plus 5% twice a year for each of three years as he asks or even five years or even more, seniors will still be so far behind that to get it even, we'd have to adjust this properly for some time." I think seniors would be very happy with an immediate 20% bump plus twice a year for three years to get caught up. My personal hope is that as seniors begin to die from lack of sustenance, that many who have suffered will not die and instead will still be around as the President makes this deficit up in six 5% payments for seniors.

In the charts that Williams has on his site, it is plain to see that the numbers do not lie like the government lies. The government lies and has illegitimate spokesmen to ask you to believe the lies.

On the average, SSR recipients in the years in which the Obama government gave zero or just about zero, the correct benefit increase based on real inflation should has been more than 6%. Hopefully a good president will examine this closely and make the right adjustments for seniors. If Biden does not effect this adjustment, would somebody please tell President Trump when he comes back that this is needed?

Before we wrap up, let's peek at the stats of the cost of living (COLA) benefits provided by the eight years Obama administration.

2009-2016 -- 2008 was from Bush

Year	COLA
2009	0%
2010	0%
2011	3.6%
2012	1.7%
2013	1.5%
2014	1.7%
2015	0%
2016	.3%

Are those numbers not pathetic? The purchasing power of seniors hit bottom during Obama's time in office. By the way, the Shadowstats true inflation using the 1980 method for 2011 is 12%. Obama's 3.6% for 2011 was way off the mark and not quite so generous as it may have first seemed.

We the people, not just seniors all lost 12% purchasing power and Mr. Obama gave seniors back 3.6%. How was that keeping with the Roosevelt deal to keep seniors whole?

I bet Mr. Barack Obama could not keep Mrs. Barack Obama's incremental budget as low as he felt seniors' spouses should keep their spouses' budget. He would have had to find another bedroom in the White-House for sleeping if he told the truth.

Chapter 14 The Big Question: Is there a Fix?

CPI has become a political tool

We have already learned that Walter J. Williams' Shadowstats uses the old-time accurate methodology using a standard market basket as a fair and honest approach to determine the real cost of living for seniors. Nothing is more intolerable in the US today than government's fraudulent taking of earned benefits, in the trillions of dollars, from seniors simply because government has the power to do so.

In an October 2015 campaign speech, Candidate Trump issued a call for wealthy Americans to "voluntarily" give up their Social Security benefits. "I have friends that are worth hundreds of millions and billions of dollars and get Social Security," he said. "They don't even know the check comes in." Trump for president said he could save money for Social Security by "getting rid of fraud."

Trump also notes that Social Security is, as he is known to say, a "deal" between Uncle Sam and American citizens and that the federal government is bound to hold up its end of the bargain. Cheating seniors for approaching forty years does not prove the case that government is keeping its side of the bargain.

"It's not unreasonable for people who paid into a system for decades to expect to get their money's worth--that's not an 'entitlement,' that's honoring a deal," he writes in his 2011 book *Time to Get Tough*.

"We as a society must also make an ironclad commitment to providing a safety net for those who can't make one for themselves. Social Security is here to stay. To be sure, we must reform it, root out the fraud, make it more efficient, and ensure that the program is solvent. Same goes for Medicare. Again, people have lived up to their end of the bargain and paid into the program in good faith...Of course they believe they're 'entitled' to receive the benefits they paid—for they are!"

Will Congress Ever Fix the CPI Problem?

Even financial experts say Trump's call to reform Social Security does have some merit.

"Surprisingly enough, Trump's few comments on Social Security could actually be the start of an effective overhaul," says Chris Carosa, a retirement specialist and author of the book, Hey! What's My Number? How to Improve the Odds You Will Retire in Comfort."

It all starts with not cutting benefits to those within 15 to 20 years of retirement -- i.e. those 50 and over -- something only Trump is adamant about."

Social Security prevents approximately 26 million seniors from falling below the poverty line each year. When anybody, especially a senior on just SSR, is on a fixed income—that right now is a mere $14,000 per year on average, there is no provision to deal with the ever-increasing costs of healthcare, prescriptions, and housing. And so, this creates a situation that breaks the promises made over 80 years ago when social security began.

Chapter 15 How to Pay for the Senior SSR Boost?

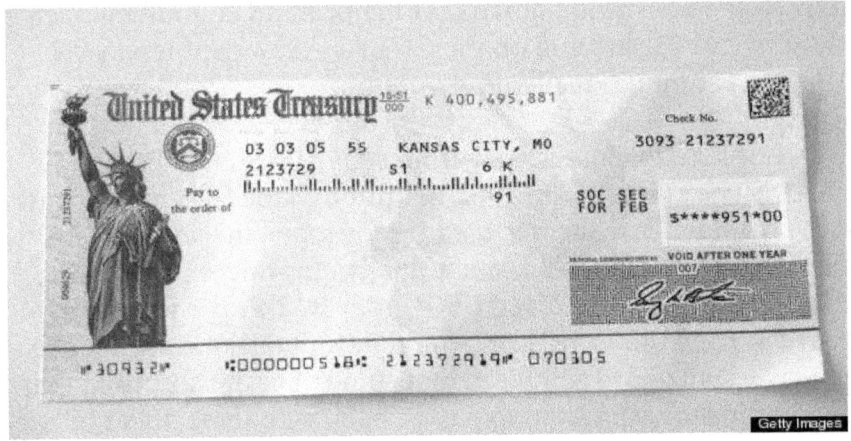

Can the US afford to pay for seniors to be OK?

First of all, the government needs to give trillions of stolen dollars back to seniors. Please do not ask again about whether the government can afford any solution to the senior crisis with COLA and Social Security. Government can do whatever it chooses. Think about the current Democrats in Congress thinking they can afford $6 Trillion for pork. That tells you they can rescue seniors from the COLA fraud and pay them back for the money the government stole.

For example, in recent years it stole a whopping $16 trillion from the treasury to pay off the big banks in the financial crisis right after Obama became president. Did the big banks ask where the money came from? No way! Seniors should not care either. Government has a million hideaways where it has more than enough to effect any solution to the senior crisis that it wishes.

Government can do whatever it wants and there is no excuse for them to not pay back seniors for raiding their social security fund and for stealing from individual seniors each and every year in the past thirty-six years.

Take note dear seniors that the US Treasury owes 65 million seniors over $2.5 Trillion dollars for major fraud committed over thirty-six years of cheating on the COLA. A few pennies a year per person per month really do mount up.

The authorities stole the money from seniors with no permission granted. Since at least from 1983 on, through the BLS bureaucrats and the contract-based coffee-breath professors, the government has been systematically and intentionally cheating seniors based on BLS-generated bastardized price indexes. To say the indexes released as the truth were fake, would be an understatement. The theft was so brazenly fraudulent that some of us are surprised that the government hasn't tried to pay us back with three dollar bills.

If this deception had not been perpetrated by the US government itself, it would be a crime punishable with a real sentence. That means that a lot of bureaucrats would be going to jail if life was fair.

It is tough to calculate the exact amount of dollars seniors have lost from this ruse. I have my own estimate. The Chapwood Index (chapwoodindex.com) gives us a good starter estimate of the total cost to seniors as they posit on their web site: "It is estimated that between 1996 and 2006, this reconfiguration of the CPI saved the US government over $680 billion." What does this mean? For one, it means that over a 10-year period, the government stole $680 billion from seniors. Considering that the miscalculations have continued for over thirty-six years, not just ten years, from 1983 to today, we can estimate the total cost.

Since 1983, according to the highly respected Chapwood Investment Group, the government has been artificially deflating the CPI to keep COLA figures for Social Security as low as possible. The government's CPI readings you see published today no longer represent the real out of pocket expenditures incurred by most Americans. It's been wrong for thirty-six years with the 1.6%

announced in October 2019 and the 1.3% from October 2020 were the 36th & 37th straight corrupt pronouncement.

The government has not ceased nor desisted in this transgression and continues to perpetuate this continual scam on the public to this very day with impunity. Very simply, the government has committed a fraud upon the people. The results of its calculations are bogus and for thirty-seven- plus years at least, they have cost seniors their annual opportunity to break-even on inflation as required by President Roosevelt's Social Security Act.

Among other tricks used to fleece seniors is the use of what is known as the corrupt baseline CPI (consumer price index). It excludes items such as taxes, energy, and food; which are not only necessities, but also often a majority of everybody's daily expenditures—especially seniors. Of course I am not suggesting that those other than seniors require no food. When food prices go up as they have for years, we know it hurts our budgets.

As previously noted, the US government saved $680 billion using fake measurements in the ten year period from 1996 to 2006. Who lost these dollars?—mostly seniors. The total period in question, however, is from 1983 to 2019—36 years. If ten years=$680 billion, then 36 years, assuming an even straight-line flow, would compute to just about $2.5 Trillion in lost inflation recompense dollars--mostly by seniors.

The purpose of the above exercise was to factually answer the question posed at the beginning of this chapter.

Can the US afford to pay for seniors to be OK?

Since every senior has been cheated every month for the past 36 years, and those seniors total approximately 65 million people, there is a big cost for the government to repay the full amount of its dishonesty. For seniors, not to be hard hearted, but that folks is not our problem. If the government did not expect to pay seniors back, it should not have stolen from us in the first place. Any fair court in the country would give us the money we deserve with interest.

The estimate above is $2.5 trillion. It is possible that the total is off a bit as it is an estimate based on incomplete work by the Chapwood Investment Group. But, I'll bet Chapwood and Shadowstats know the real number and I would make a bet it is more than $2.5 trillion.

Through my request, which I have repeated several times in this book, seniors are not asking for every dollar stolen to come back with interest. We are asking for less but it will be an amount that will make a major difference in the lives of most seniors. Those who are well-to-do-and choose not to receive the recompense may request that they not be included with our thank you's, of course. I would encourage those who do not need to take this, to let those that need it be the beneficiaries.

The amount confiscated at a 5% to 10% rate each and every year for 36 years from seniors without permission is enormous. In 1983, thirty-six years ago, about 40 million seniors collected Social Security payments. This year, the number is about 65 million. To know the extent of the theft from all seniors, you would have to take the fraudulent COLA given from the proper COLA that should have been given and multiply it by the number collecting. Like I said, it is an enormous number. That is why we rounded it all up using the Chapwood index using a ten year period from Chapwood as our base. That number is $2.5 Trillion.

My point is the US stole this money dollar by dollar, payment by payment, year by year times the number of people cheated. So, as you can see, not only can the US afford to pay what is due, it is not a choice. It is recompense for a theft by the government of extremely large sums of money taken a couple bucks at a time. Nobody expects seniors to fund the government.

The United States cannot afford _not_ to do what is right. This is America! If we could afford to give the biggest banks a $16 trillion bailout and we can afford $6 Trillion in the Democrat pork budget in 2021, we can afford to fix social security and give seniors a make-up payment that lets them keep their houses and keep them out of the poorhouse. You remember the big bank bailouts around the time Bush was exiting and Obama was taking the oath. What is owed seniors is a very small percentage of that.

There are lots of other ways to pay for a recompense for seniors, but first the government must accept publicly that they (what's that proper word that can be used in place of screwed) seniors for so many years, many seniors forgot they were getting it handed to them.

The noticeable symptom for seniors was that all of a sudden after years of cumulative thievery by the government, seniors could no longer keep up with their expenses. This would not have happened if constant dollars were used as promised in the legislation. The government cheated—plain and simple. they could not keep their hands off the people's money with which they were entrusted.

Lots has been written about the government's money (our money) bailing out corporations and big banks. Petrino DiLeo on September 7, 2011 after the bailout notion was really settling in and somehow was accepted, wrote how Wall Street banks are still not finished raking in taxpayer dollars. This paragraph gives his perspective:

> "While the media focused on the Washington charade over raising the federal debt ceiling and cutting the estimated budget deficit, a "a one-time audit of the Federal Reserve released in late July" showed that the Treasury Department and Federal Reserve Bank have doled out an incredible $16 trillion in assistance to financial institutions and corporations in the U.S. and around the world."

Did anybody ask where that money came from?

Seniors should not even try to tell the government where to get the money to make the pay back. The money guys in the government already know where to find it.

If somebody says we cannot afford to assure that seniors can lead lives in which the poorhouse is not a constant threat, please tell them to remember the promise of Franklin D. Roosevelt about constant dollars for those collecting Social Security. Certainly not one dollar should be paid in welfare to illegal aliens if ever, until seniors receive their rightful benefits back pay.

I have confidence that OMB Director Mick Mulvaney is as sharp as a tack. He is so good with numbers, he can look everywhere to find a way to make seniors whole and like Trump says, make the benefits means tested so that billionaires do not collect unless they insist they be paid. Then we publish their names. We can afford making senior citizens on SSR whole again; and we must. We're smart enough to get the job done.

Today's Social Security dilemma began after Lyndon Johnson permitted the SSR Trust Fund to be robbed to pay for his social welfare programs in the late 1960's.

Then sometime in the 1980's the dirtiest politicians in America colluded with coffee-breath professors in academe so they would not have to take the real cost of living into consideration when calculating the percentage increase in senior's benefits, AKA COLA.

They contrived notions such as CPI-U, CPI-W, and the Chained CPI—all schemes to reduce COLA and return dollars to the treasury from the backs of senior citizens.

All SSR recipients wanted was what Roosevelt promised. They wanted to be paid in constant dollars. None of the CPI machinations do that and none ever did that, and until the President and Congress orders the BLS to calculate inflation using the real market basket technique and not those invented to cheat seniors, the elderly will never get to ever see a constant dollar.

None of these BLS contrivances were intended to provide the true cost of living and /or the true out of pocket expense increases endured by senior citizens who were fortunate enough to that point to be able to survive in America despite losing money each year.

Nobody in America other than the Bureau of Labor Statistics (BLS) and coffee breath professors in academe want this perpetration to stand, especially seniors who face record foreclosures and the terrible decisions about whether to eat or buy their prescription medicine. Government employees do not know the plight they have created for seniors. What would they do if they faced the threat of losing their homes or they had to scrape to find their next substantial meal?

I am sure the President and the few members of Congress who represent the people can handle the deep thinking to pull this reversal off in the right way. Remember, the dollars are owed to seniors. This is not a gift.

Maybe it would be OK if seniors were paid back more than needed but I am not suggesting that. The fact is these make-up COLAs of 10% every half-year for three years can certainly be paid from sources known only to the government.

I can recall as he ran for the presidency, then Mr. Trump said that the US had enough oil in the ground to pay off the national debt. My suggestion is to first take care of the cheated seniors and then go back and pay off the national debt. Why not? The government owes seniors much more than my recommendation for a proper payback amount and a social security system reset.

Going back to Trump's campaign braggadocio, it helps to remember that Donald Trump once said that he could pay off the national debt with the oil reserves that are in this country. Using new estimates that prove that the US has more reserves than any other country—at least 264 billion barrels, we are sitting on a lot of black gold with much of it on public lands.

I do not want to tap it today for the full seniors' payback. I do not care where the money comes from. However, I will not permit anybody who hates seniors to poor-mouth me about the US running out of money anytime soon. And, please do not dare to say this country cannot pay back seniors for the involuntary sacrifice we made for over 36 years. Who was going to give the Democrats the $6 Trillion in this year's budget? Take care of US seniors first.

From verified calculations, it is now fact that seniors on SSR are owed about $4.5 dollars for every dollar in benefits received in their monthly e-checks. Seniors therefore receive $3.50 less than due against each dollar they receive because of the inherent fraud in the new versions of the CPI as perpetrated by our very own national government.

Seniors are not greedy and therefore do not need to be paid in full all at once. A 10% per year COLA every six months three full years (six COLA bumps altogether before the SSR reset), would go a long way in getting seniors back on track. In my opinion, and by now it is surely your opinion also, this is a debt due from theft by government. It is not a gift.

The cost of providing Social Security benefits is huge at about $900 billion per year. Providing a semiannual 10% make-up COLA for seniors beginning in 2021, and continuing to 2024 to start can be handled by a combination of cost savings and revenue from oil and from the great mind of a calculator like Mick Mulvaney. .

The oil reserve is a major bonanza. I have another way in which a $Trillion per year can be saved in immigration costs but I would prefer to release the notes on how to do this when I put out my next book on how to solve the immigration crisis the American way. There is enough money to be saved on immigration to pay most of the senior debt.

My point is that there are a zillion ways to fund the senior payback. As an aside, with appropriate legislation, a 10% tax on oil extraction can keep Social Security going forever with seniors again being able to afford a nice steak every now and then and maybe even a Lobster Tail on New Year's Eve.

One of my objectives for the senior payback and the system reset is that seniors stop eating cat tuna even if the BLS and the coffee-breath professors in academe suggest it. For my two-cents, I would like to see cat tuna companies going bankrupt when their only clients begin again to include only the cat population. Meanwhile seniors will be eating balanced meals. Doesn't that sound right?

FYI, the word *"screwed"* in informal settings does not necessarily have any sexual connotations. Screwed in fact means a *hopeless situation; ruined or broken.* That describes the plight of seniors because of government pilferage.

My job in this book is to point out to seniors that we have been *"screwed"* by nobody else regarding social security than our own government and we deserve to be paid back now. The government stole from us.

Therefore, we cannot sit back and wait for the problem to rectify itself. We must insist that the government cease and desist from stealing any more. Calculate the fair and true cost of inflation and use it. And, of course the government must pay us all back for what they stole—at least a significant portion thereof. It is only right.

Without a major action by the president (things can then happen overnight), our biggest problem seems to be that our politicians are not sure if they want to be honest or not. Seniors can solve that one also by not sending these scoundrels back into office.

If our politicians had the political will to do the right thing, we would not have to threaten their jobs. Unfortunately, politicians think they are above the people they serve, and remain reluctant to do the right thing. So, what should we do?

Can you imagine the savings we can amass when we discover that there are 60 million, not 11 million illegal aliens who live in America? If we cut off the funding for that other government boondoggle—paying the ride for non-Americans, there should be a few dollars to not only pay back seniors but also provide some reparations—not that we are asking for reparations.

The thing that I would recommend for seniors to do after reading this book is to not just get out the bottle and have a few swills to calm down the depression. That would be OK, but after one day of swilling to drown the sorrows of the past, seniors must move on to the future.

We can solve this and make it work for us. Even bigger than millennials, we are the biggest singular voting bloc in the country with a ton of almost seniors in our on-deck circle—just waiting to collect their share of a pie that must not be made smaller by cheating bureaucrats.

The time for seniors sitting back, taking it on the chin, wringing their hands and saying *what can I do* are over. We must get energized; write cards and letters to our representatives and the president and write letters to the editor. Perhaps a few senior demonstrations would be good exercise for us all.

I am seeing more signs that something good can happen if we stay at it. For example, we now have Congressmen writing letters hoping to get other Congressmen to begin working on behalf of seniors

Here is a letter from Congressman John Garamendi (D-CA-3). The title of his public letter written to the Seniors League on April 30, 2019 is "Its Time for Seniors to Get a Fair COLA." He sure is right but will his activity end with this letter. I hope not.

> Social Security benefits and cost-of-living adjustments (COLA) specifically, have not kept up with inflation. Americans everywhere agree: Social Security is not an entitlement; it is a benefit that seniors earn through decades of work serving our nation's economy. According to the Social Security Administration, approximately 63 million Americans received Social Security benefits in 2018, and of those 63 million, 72% were retired workers and dependents.

Garamendi notes that in 2017, seniors received a mere 0.3% COLA increase to their benefits. 2016 was even worse. For just the third time since Social Security was created, Americas seniors received no cost-of-living adjustment at all in 2016. However, in 2018, with Trump's first COLA, we saw the highest COLA in years: 2.8%. This is the largest increase since 2012, and we must continue this upward trend.

He went on to explain the CPI-W and how it is designed to stiff seniors. He noted that according to The Senior Citizens League, recipients of Social Security have seen a 34% decrease in their buying power since 2000. Other indexes say the loss is even greater. He also complains about seniors who are enrolled in Medicare Part B programs, having faced very large cost increases. He says it is simply unacceptable and that is why it needs to change. So, he is introducing the Fair COLA for Seniors Act.

This is a great idea for a start. Seniors, however, are already so far behind the eight-ball that they need action like I recommend in this chapter. Both a payback and a reset to an inflation-based system.

Garamendi says that it is unfair and unjust to expect American seniors to settle for a COLA that is less than what they have spent their entire lives working for. This is why it is critical to base COLAs on an index that reflects what seniors actually spend their money on. It is time for Congress to take action and give our nation's seniors what they deserve.

It sure is. Thank you Congressman Garamendi. Now, please go to the Congressional Cocktail Lounge and start talking to you buddies—both Democrats and Republican and go get something done for real instead of talking about it.

Chapter 16 Senior Solution Review: Pay Back the Big Rip-Off

Mike Huckabee is for seniors

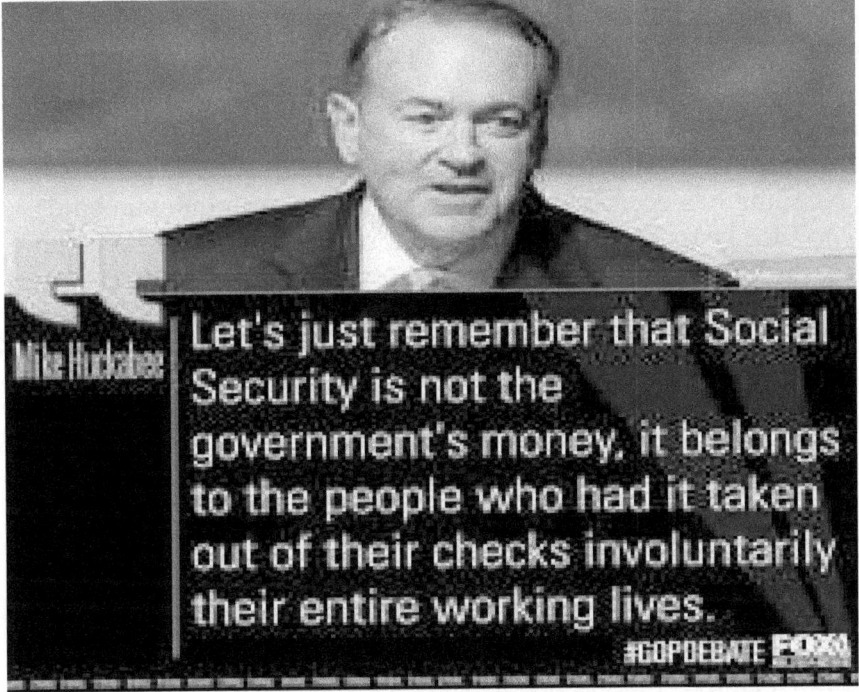

When the Republican debates began, Mike Huckabee, a person who is tough to dislike, was the first brave Republican to complain when he publicly accused "illegals, prostitutes, pimps, (and) drug dealers" of freeloading off the Social Security system during the first GOP primary debate way back on August. 6, 2015.

I have a big book here and it is finished after this last chapter. If you get nothing out of this book besides the notions in this paragraph and the next, it will be worth my writing it. Our government in its present composition does not deserve our trust. Senior Citizens, I regret, choose not to complain about bad things that "happen" to them as Mike Huckabee did in the cutout above and in his quote repeated here:

Mike Huckabee as you may recall was the first brave Republican in the 2016 debates to complain when he publicly accused: *"illegals, prostitutes, pimps, (and) drug dealers"* of freeloading off the Social Security system He did not add *"with the permission of the Democrat Party"* but it would have been just as true if he had.

The government will not admit nor publish the costs registered in the SSR system that are caused by generous government workers out in the field certifying illegals as eligible.

Mike Huckabee knows the truth as do many other politicos, who, unlike Huckabee, choose to do nothing to help America. This freeloading has been free to everybody but the seniors who paid the toll for years. We should all count on President Trump when he assumes power again to repay seniors well for all the past pilferage. Seniors are in need and when Trump reads this book, he will know what he must do to solve the problem permanently for seniors when he is back in office. Of course we have to get him back into the driver's seat again.

Will Trump keep his word?

We love to remind the former president that during his campaign, candidate Trump promised to protect Social Security without cutting benefits. I wrote this book to help remind seniors as well as our 45th and 47th President that protecting SSR is a great notion that must be done with sharp teeth and of course, with a handsome presidential smile. The president is not permitted to renege on his word. We the seniors of America need him big time on this one. If Joe Biden wants to help, his help right now would be most welcome.

In fact, seniors need lots more than smiles or the status quo that put them behind what's fair over the last thirty-six years or so. The President's team knows full well that seniors should be receiving $4.50 for every 1983 (maybe even 1975) dollar received today. It is a fact. Chalk it up to the ravages of inflation. Seniors should not be singled out to pay this great nation's total cost of inflation.

I will say it again as some seniors may still be unbelieving. This message must be repeated and repeated. Senior citizens have been cheated and need to be paid back for the abuses to the system affecting them first-hand over the years. They cost each senior tens of thousands of dollars—enough to buy back the house they lost, perhaps. It is not pennies.

Mike Huckabee and other brave Americans have cited these. It is an obligation of America through President Trump and President Biden to make seniors whole again.

The obligation includes paying back Medicare from Obamacare and by increasing SSR benefits over the next eight years (at least three years) of the two Trump terms by at least 10% semi-annually for the next three years. After three years of 10% COLA every six months, it would still not make seniors whole. It would be only half or so of what is owed. Most seniors would, however, be well on their way to a renaissance of life without major debt.

Seniors still believe Donald Trump is the real deal. So do I but I worry sometimes. We can't let the Democrats cheat him out of another election and we have to clean Congress of the Democrats who do not care one iota about the well-being of senior citizens. It would be wonderful if President Trump got eight years in total (4 & 4 or better if he is called back) and he kept the flow of benefit increases so that when he departs six years or so from now. seniors will be brought back almost whole and the CPI will no longer be a hocus-pocus calculation made by people who do not care.

A Nice Closing Thought—I Hope

How do we acknowledge the contributions older people have made and continue to make to our society? In 1963, President John F. Kennedy designated May as "senior citizens Month" the precursor to the current name "Older Americans Month." During the month of May, the current president formally addressed the country asking the citizens to pay tribute to the elderly in their communities. In honor of this request, Diversity Best Practices has compiled a list of key organizations that serve older Americans. There is also a theme to every Older American Month celebration – in 2015 the theme was "Get into the Act."

No senior was a senior all his or her life. In fact some seniors do not even feel like they are seniors and we instinctively speak of seniors in the third person.

I figure since this is the last couple paragraphs in the book, I ought to admit that as we close out this book about no longer *"screwing"* senior citizens and making senior citizens whole again as we should be, I should admit that I speak from authority. I waited until a month before I was 64 to go on Social Security. When the first "check" came, I was absolutely thrilled.

I am now 74 years old but when I talk about seniors, I admit that I feel like I am talking about others – not me. May God bless all senior citizens and may we all decide to fight against those who would take our livelihood away—especially corrupt BLS bureaucrats and coffee-breath professors. Amen!

Hopefully the current president and former President Trump both hear my plea to give all seniors a true payback from government theft of the past as well as a promise that nothing other than true inflation will set the constant inflation rate announced in 1935 in the SSA Act and most certainly as expected by President Roosevelt.

God bless all seniors and may God bless America—and keep her great!

Other Books by Brian W. Kelly: (amazon.com, and Kindle)

Larry Elder Governor of California. Perfect candidate for California
WineDiets.Com Renews: The Wine Diet Includes three wine diets & an alcohol-free diet
Katie Kelly & Her Miracle Voice Singer, Songwriter, Musician and Producer
Beating Big Tech Monopolies! Just like when the Trustbusters beat the robber-barons in 1900s
The Great Story of Florida Gators Football Beginning of football to the Coach Dan Mullen's era
The Great Story of LSU Football The beginning of football to the Ed Orgeron era
The Great Story of Clemson Football Starts at the first football game to the Dabo Swinney era
The Great Story of Alabama Football From the first college football game to Alabama's last TD u
The Great Story of Notre Dame Football The beginning of football to coach Brian Kelly's last game
The Great Story of Penn State Football From the beginning of football to the last James Franklin game
Great Moments in College Football From the beginning of football to the 2020 post season.
Great Players in Tampa Bay Buccaneers Football From the beginning of football through the Bruce Ariens era
Super Bowl & NFL Championship Seasons: The Tampa Bay Buccaneers First championship to Super B
Great Coaches in Tampa Bay Buccaneers Football Begins continues through the Bruce Ariens era.
Great Moments in Tampa Bay Buccaneers Football Begins beginning of Football to Bruce Ariens era.
Donald Trump Governor of California After the Newsom recall, Trump is the perfect candidate
Ron DeSantis: The Best United States Governor To Governors what Trump is to Presidents—The Best!
Mike v Trump: Mike Grant takes on Donald Trump; Brian Kelly takes on Mike Grant;
SCOTUS Eliminatus No country needs a Supreme Court that refuses to hear critical cases!
The Corruption in the WB Area School District A Story about toxic corruption and other stinky things
Stolen Election ???   Democrats say: "fair and just;" Republicans surrender to Democrats
The Ten Commandments of Calipered Kinematically Aligned Total Knee Arthroplasty Color
The Ten Commandments of Calipered Kinematically Aligned Total Knee Arthroplasty B/W
About Alexa! Tell me how!
Chronicle of Inept Governance & Corrective Actions board from hell big question: better way?
Hey Alexa Create me my own personal musical paradise Unpublished with new book
FTC Case: LetsGoPublish.com v Amazon   Fourth Edition big bully censored nine books
FTC Case: LetsGoPublish.com v Amazon   Third Edition big bully censored nine books
FTC Case: LetsGoPublish.com v Amazon   Second Edition big bully censored nine books
The President Donald J. Trump Book Catalog   Color Version by Brian Kelly & Lets Go Publish!
The President Donald J. Trump Book Catalog   B/W Version by Brian Kelly & Lets Go Publish!
FTC Case: LetsGoPublish.com v Amazon   Original case bully censored nine books
What America Wins if Biden Wins Everything!!!!!! The answer is really nothing.
What America Loses if Trump Loses None of the 1000s of Trump wins for starters
What America Wins When Trump Wins Trump already gave the country more benefits and blessings
We Love Trump! Don't you? The President given to the people by God as the answer to our prayers
Amazon: The Biggest Bully in Town bully blocked eight books in 2020 by most published author
Trump Assured 2020 Victory President needs these two prongs for his platform for landslide
2020 Republican Convention—Speeches Blocked by Amazon Includes memento free Link
2020 RNC Convention Full Speech Transcripts   Blocked by Amazon Memento of the 87 best
COVID-19 Mask, Yes? Or No? It's Everybody's Recommended Solution!!!
LSU Tigers Championship Seasons Starts at beginning of LSU Football to the National Championship
Great Coaches in LSU Football Book starts with the first LSU coach; goes to Orgeron Championship
Great Players in LSU Football Begins with 1893 QB Ruffin G Pleasant to 2019 QB Burrow
America for Millennials A growing # of disintegrationists want to tear US down
Great Moments in LSU Football   Book starts at start of Football to the Ed Orgeron Championship.
The Constitution's Role in a Return to Normalcy Can the Constitution Survive?
The Constitution vs. The Virus Simultaneous attack coronavirus and US governors
One, Two, Three, Pooph!!! Reopen Country Now! Return to normalcy is just around the corner.
Reopen America Now Return to Normalcy
Enough is Enough Re: Covid, We are not children. We're adults. We'll make the right decisions.
How to Write Your 1st Book & Publish it Using Amazon KDP You can do it
REMDESIVIR A Ray of Hope
When Will America Reopen for Business? This author's opinion includes voices of experts
HydroxyChloroquine: The Game Changer
Super Bowl & NFL Championship Seasons The KC Chiefs From the 1st to Super Bowl LIV
Great Coaches in Kansas City Chiefs Football First Coach era to Andy Reid Era
Great Players in Kansas City Chiefs Football From the AFL to Andy Reid Era
Reopen America Now! How to Shut-Down Corona Virus & Return to Normalcy!
Why is Everybody Moving to the Villages? You can afford a home in the Villages
CORONAVIRUS The Cause & the Cure. Many solutions—but which ones will work?

168 Social Security Screw Job

Great Moments in Kansas City Chiefs Football. From the beginning to the Andy Reid Era
How the Philadelphia Eagles Lost Its Karma. This is the one place that tells the story
Cancel All Student Debt Now! Good for America, Good for the Economy.
Social Security Screw Job!!! Scandal: Seniors Intentionally Screwed by US Government
Trump Hate They hate Trump Supporters; Trump; & God—in that order
Christmas Wings for Brian A heartwarming story of a boy whose shoulders kept growing
Merry Christmas to Wilkes-Barre 50 Ways" for Mayor George Brown to Create a Better City.
Air Force Football Championship Seasons From AF Championship to Coach Calhoun's latest team
Syracuse Football Championship Seasons beginning of SU championships; goes to Dino Babers Era
Navy Football Championship Seasons 1st Navy Championships to the Ken Niumatalolo Era
Army Football Championship Seasons Beginning of Football championships to Jeff Monken Era
Florida Gators Championship Seasons Beginning of Football through championships to Dan Mullen era
Alabama's Championship Seasons Beginning of Football past the 2017/2018 National Championship
Clemson Tigers Championship Seasons Beginning of Football to the Clemson National Championships
Penn State's Championship Seasons PSU's first championship to the James Franklin era
Notre Dame's Championship Seasons Before Knute Rockne and past Lou Holtz's 1988 undisputed title
Super Bowls & Championship Seasons: The New York Giants Many championships of the Giants.
Super Bowls & Championship Seasons: New England Patriots Many championships of the Patriots.
Super Bowls & Championship Seasons: The Pittsburgh Steelers Many championship of the Steelers
Super Bowls & Championship Seasons: The Philadelphia Eagles Many championships of the Eagles.
The Big Toxic School Wilkes-Barre Area's Tale of Corruption, Deception, Taxation & Tyranny
Great Players in New York Giants Football Begins with great players of 1925 to the Saquon Barqley era.
Great Coaches in New York Giants Football Begins with Bob Folwell 1925 and to Pat Shurmur in 2019.
Great Moments in New York Giants Football Beginning of Football to the Pat Shurmur era.
Hasta La Vista California Give California its independence.
IT's ALL OVER! Mueller: NO COLLUSION!"—Top Dems going to jail for the hoax!
Democrat Secret for Power & Winning Elections Open borders adds millions of new Democrat Voters
Hope for Wilkes-Barre—John Q. Doe—Next Mayor of Wilkes-Barre
The John Doe Plan & WB Plan will help create a better city!
Great Moments in New England Patriots Football Second Edition
This book begins at the beginning of Football and goes to the Bill Belichick era.
The Cowardly Congress Corrupt US Congress is against America and Americans.
Great Players in Air Force Football From the beginning to the current season
Great Coaches in Air Force Football From the beginning to Coach Troy Calhoun
Help for Mayor George and Next Mayor of Wilkes-Barre How to vote for the next Mayor Council
Ghost of Wilkes-Barre Future: Spirit's advice for residents how to pick the next Mayor and Council
Great Players in Air Force Football: Air Force's best players of all time
Great Coaches in Air Force Football: From Coach 1 to Coach Troy Calhoun
Great Moments in Air Force Football: From day 1 to today
Great Players in Navy Football: Navy's best including Bellino & Staubach
Great Coaches in Navy. Football: From Coach 1 to Coach #39 Ken Niumatalolo
Great Moments in Navy Football: From day 1 to coach Ken Niumatalolo l
No Tree! No Toys! No Toot! Heartwarming story. Christmas gone while 19 month old napped
How to End DACA, Sanctuary Cities, & Resident Illegal Aliens . best solution remove shadows America.
Government Must Stop Ripping Off Seniors' Social Security!: Hey buddy, seniors can't spare a dime?
Special Report: Solving America's Student Debt Crisis!: The only real solution to the $1.52 Trillion debt
The Winning Political Platform for America Unique winning approach to solve big problems in America.
Lou Barletta v Bob Casey for US Senate   Barletta's unique approach to solve big problems in America.
John Chrin v Matt Cartwright for Congress Chrin has a unique approach to solve big problems in America.
The Cure for Hate !!! Can the cure be any worse than this disease that is crippling America?
Andrew Cuomo's Time to Go? He Was Never that Great!": Cuomo says America never that great
White People Are Bad! Bad! Bad! Whoever thought a popular slogan in 2018 It's OK to be White!
The Fake News Media Is Also Corrupt !!!: Fake press / media today is not worthy to be 4th Estate.
God Gave US Donald Trump?   Trump was sent from God as the people's answer
Millennials Say America Was Never That Great": Too many pleased days of political chumps not over!
It's Time for The John Q. Doe Party... Don't you think? By Elephants.
Great Players in Florida Gators Football... Tim Tebow and a ton of other great players
Great Coaches in Florida Gators Football... The best coaches in Gator history.
The Constitution by Hamilton, Jefferson, Madison, et al. The Real Constitution
The Constitution Companion. Will help you learn and understand the Constitution
Great Coaches in Clemson Football The best Clemson Coaches right to Dabo Swinney
Great Players in Clemson Football The best Clemson players in history
Winning Back America. America's been stolen and can be won back completely
The Founding of America... Great book to pick up a lot of great facts

Defeating America's Career Politicians. The scoundrels need to go.
Midnight Mass by Jack Lammers… You remember what it was like Great story
The Bike by Jack Lammers… Great heartwarming Story by Jack
Wipe Out All Student Loan Debt--Now! Watch the economy go boom!
No Free Lunch Pay Back Welfare! Why not pay it back?
Deport All Millennials Now!!! Why they deserve to be deported and/or saved
DELETE the EPA, Please! The worst decisions to hurt America
Taxation Without Representation 4th Edition Should we throw the TEA overboard again?
Four Great Political Essays by Thomas Dawson
Top Ten Political Books for 2018… Cliffsnotes Version of 10 Political Books
Top Six Patriotic Books for 2018… Cliffsnotes version of 6 Patriotic Boosk
Why Trump Got Elected!.. It's great to hear about a great milestone in America!
The Day the Free Press Died. Corrupt Press Lives on!
Solved (Immigration) The best solutions for 2018
Solved II (Obamacare, Social Security, Student Debt) Check it out; They're solved.
Great Moments in Pittsburgh Steelers Football... Six Super Bowls and more.
Great Players in Pittsburgh Steelers Football ,,,Chuck Noll, Bill Cowher, Mike Tomin, etc.
Great Coaches in New England Patriots Football,,, Bill Belichick the one and only plus others
Great Players in New England Patriots Football… Tom Brady, Drew Bledsoe et al.
Great Coaches in Philadelphia Eagles Football. Andy Reid, Doug Pederson & Lots more
Great Players in Philadelphia Eagles Football Great players such as Sonny Jurgenson
Great Coaches in Syracuse Football All the greats including Ben Schwartzwalder
Great Players in Syracuse Football. Highlights best players such as Jim Brown & Donovan McNabb
Millennials are People Too !!! Give US millennials help to live American Dream
Brian Kelly for the United States Senate from PA: Fresh Face for US Senate
The Candidate's Bible. Don't pray for your campaign without this bible
Rush Limbaugh's Platform for Americans… Rush will love it
Sean Hannity's Platform for Americans… Sean will love it
Donald Trump's New Platform for Americans. Make Trump unbeatable in 2020
Tariffs Are Good for America! One of the best tools a president can have
Great Coaches in Pittsburgh Steelers Football Sixteen of the best coaches ever to coach in pro football.
Great Moments in New England Patriots Football Great football moments from Boston to New England
Great Moments in Philadelphia Eagles Football. The best from the Eagles from the beginning of football.
Great Moments in Syracuse Football The great moments, coaches & players in Syracuse Football
Boost Social Security Now! Hey Buddy, Can You Spare a Dime?
The Birth of American Football. From the first college game in 1869 to the last Super Bowl
Obamacare: A One-Line Repeal Congress must get this done.
A Wilkes-Barre Christmas Story A wonderful town makes Christmas all the better
A Boy, A Bike, A Train, and a Christmas Miracle A Christmas story that will melt your heart
Pay-to-Go   America-First Immigration Fix
Legalizing Illegal Aliens Via Resident Visas Americans-first plan saves $Trillions. Learn how!
60 Million Illegal Aliens in America!!! A simple, America-first solution.
The Bill of Rights By Founder James Madison Refresh your knowledge of the specific rights for all
Great Players in Army Football Great Army Football played by great players..
Great Coaches in Army Football Army's coaches are all great.
Great Moments in Army Football Army Football at its best.
Great Moments in Florida Gators Football Gators Football from the start. This is the book.
Great Moments in Clemson Football CU Football at its best. This is the book.
Great Moments in Florida Gators Football Gators Football from the start. This is the book.
The Constitution Companion. A Guide to Reading and Comprehending the Constitution
The Constitution by Hamilton, Jefferson, & Madison – Big type and in English
PATERNO: The Dark Days After Win # 409. Sky began to fall within days of win # 409.
JoePa 409 Victories: Say No More! Winningest Division I-A football coach ever
American College Football: The Beginning From before day one football was played.
Great Coaches in Alabama Football Challenging the coaches of every other program!
Great Coaches in Penn State Football the Best Coaches in PSU's football program
Great Players in Penn State Football The best players in PSU's football program
Great Players in Notre Dame Football The best players in ND's football program
Great Coaches in Notre Dame Football The best coaches in any football program
Great Players in Alabama Football from Quarterbacks to offensive Linemen Greats!
Great Moments in Alabama Football AU Football from the start. This is the book.
Great Moments in Penn State Football PSU Football, start--games, coaches, players,
Great Moments in Notre Dame Football ND Football, start, games, coaches, players

Cross Country with the Parents A great trip from East Coast to West with the kids
Seniors, Social Security & the Minimum Wage. Things seniors need to know.
How to Write Your First Book and Publish It with CreateSpace. You too can be an author.
The US Immigration Fix--It's all in here. Finally, an answer.
I had a Dream IBM Could be #1 Again The title is self-explanatory
WineDiets.Com Presents The Wine Diet Learn how to lose weight while having fun.
Wilkes-Barre, PA; Return to Glory Wilkes-Barre City's return to glory
Geoffrey Parsons' Epoch... The Land of Fair Play Better than the original.
The Bill of Rights 4 Dummmies! This is the best book to learn about your rights.
Sol Bloom's Epoch ...Story of the Constitution The best book to learn the Constitution
America 4 Dummmies! All Americans should read to learn about this great country.
The Electoral College 4 Dummmies! How does it really work?
The All-Everything Machine Story about IBM's finest computer server.
ThankYou IBM! This book explains how IBM was beaten in the computer marketplace by neophytes

Amazon.com/author/brianwkelly
Brian W. Kelly has written 295 books including this book.
Thanks again for buying this one.

Other Books by Brian W. Kelly

CPSIA information can be obtained
at www.ICGtesting.com
Printed in the USA
BVHW040100230422
635022BV00007B/145